T0339522

Cambridge Elements ☰

Elements in the Philosophy of Religion
edited by
Yujin Nagasawa
University of Birmingham

ENTAILMENT, CONTRADICTION, AND CHRISTIAN THEISM

Jc Beall
University of Notre Dame

Michael DeVito
University of Birmingham

CAMBRIDGE
UNIVERSITY PRESS

Shaftesbury Road, Cambridge CB2 8EA, United Kingdom

One Liberty Plaza, 20th Floor, New York, NY 10006, USA

477 Williamstown Road, Port Melbourne, VIC 3207, Australia

314–321, 3rd Floor, Plot 3, Splendor Forum, Jasola District Centre, New Delhi – 110025, India

103 Penang Road, #05–06/07, Visioncrest Commercial, Singapore 238467

Cambridge University Press is part of Cambridge University Press & Assessment, a department of the University of Cambridge.

We share the University's mission to contribute to society through the pursuit of education, learning and research at the highest international levels of excellence.

www.cambridge.org
Information on this title: www.cambridge.org/9781108995429
DOI: 10.1017/9781108995788

First published 2023

A catalogue record for this publication is available from the British Library.

ISBN 978-1-108-99542-9 Paperback
ISSN 2399-5165 (online)
ISSN 2515-9763 (print)

Entailment, Contradiction, and Christian Theism

Elements in the Philosophy of Religion

DOI: 10.1017/9781108995788
First published online: March 2023

Jc Beall
University of Notre Dame

Michael DeVito
University of Birmingham

Author for correspondence: Jc Beall, JBeall@ND.edu

Abstract: Apparent contradiction is common in traditional monotheism, and perhaps especially so in standard christian theology given central doctrines such as the incarnation and trinity. This Element aims to chart out a very elementary but abstract framework through which such contradictions may be approached. It does not attempt to address the many options for thinking about contradictions in the face of logical entailment; it charts only a few salient abstract options.

Keywords: christian theism, contradiction, gluts, incarnation, trinity

ISBNs: 9781108995429 (PB), 9781108995788 (OC)
ISSNs: 2399-5165 (online), 2515-9763 (print)

Contents

Introduction

The aim of this discussion is to chart salient but abstract responses to apparent contradiction in christian theology. The chart is drawn as simply, concisely, and minimally as possible compatible with user-friendliness. Along these lines, the focus is on abstract responses to contradiction versus historically occupied responses, although, where appropriate, pointers to possible historical occupants of canvassed positions are provided.

One motivation behind spelling out the abstract framework – and illustrating over and again with different examples – is to highlight the need for theologians and theology-focused philosophers to spell out the entailment relations that are inexorably involved in their would-be responses to theological contradiction. Theology, at least qua truth-seeking theory, aims at a would-be true theory of theological reality. 'Systematic' theologies cannot be adequately evaluated or even understood without spelling out at least a few of the basic entailment relations that govern them.

Our hope is that this Element provides an abstract framework through which theology-directed work may identify – and precisely spell out – at least the basic entailment relations on which their would-be theories (i.e., theologies) rest.

One final administrative note: as mentioned, we aim to be very concise, providing tools and basic illustrations – and nothing more. Minimal but adequate references towards actual theories (however loosely spelled out) are cited for purposes of pointing interested readers towards sufficient bibliographies.

TOOLS, TERMINOLOGY, AND BASIC IDEAS
1 Entailment, Contradiction, and Theories

The terminology of 'contradiction' is closely related to that of 'entailment' and 'consequence'. These terms are defined, for present purposes, as follows.

1.1 Entailment

An *entailment relation* is a lack-of-counterexample relation between sentences of a language. Here, counterexamples are 'possibilities' recognized by the given relation. For example, while there are logical possibilities in which the actual physical laws are broken by physical objects, such possibilities are not recognized as physical possibilities – or genuine counterexamples – by the entailment relation(s) governing true physics. While there are logical possibilities in which polytheism is true, such merely logical possibilities are not treated as genuine theological possibilities by standard christian theological theory; they are not genuine counterexamples to the theological necessity of monotheism. The point, for present purposes, is that refutation of a would-be entailment claim demands a counterexample (viz., a relevant possibility in which the would-be *entailing* sentences are true but the would-be *entailed* sentence is untrue); however, the counterexample needs to be one that is recognized within – or within the range of or scope of – the target entailment claim (i.e., in the range of the target entailment relation). Again, pointing to logical possibilities in which physics is different from true (actual) physical theory is irrelevant if such merely logical possibilities aren't recognized as physical possibilities by the entailment relation of true physics.

Let R be an entailment relation in the foregoing sense, say, the entailment relation over all physical possibilities, or the entailment relation over all theological possibilities, or so on. When a sentence A of the relevant language (e.g., the language of physics, or of theology, or etc.) R-entails a sentence B of the language (i.e., A entails B according to the relation R), the sentence B is said to be a *consequence* of sentence A *according to R*. Example: in standard christian theology, the sentence 'Christ is holy' is a *consequence* of the sentence 'Christ is divine', since, according to standard christian theology, the divinity of a person entails the holiness of the person. There may be logical possibilities in which divinity and holiness come apart, but those logical possibilities are not relevant possibilities – and, hence, not relevant counterexamples – to the given entailment claim from divinity to holiness, at least according to the entailment relation involved in standard christian theology.

Further illustration of such terms is provided in subsequent sections wherein the terms are put to use. The definitions of target terms run as follows.

Definition 1 (Entailment relation: sentence–sentence) *Let A and B be sentences of some language. A entails B according to relation R (equivalently, A R-entails B) iff there's no relevant possibility in which A is true but B untrue.*

Definition 2 (Entailment relation: set–sentence) *Let X be a set of sentences of some language, say, $\{A_1, \ldots, A_n\}$, and let B be a sentence of the given language. X entails B according to entailment relation R iff there is no relevant possibility in which all elements of X are true but B untrue.*

1.2　Some Special Entailment Relations

Logical entailment is a special relation in the sense that it's universal and topic-neutral. This is the entailment relation over all 'logical possibilities', the broadest set of possibilities, governing the very sparse set of so-called logical vocabulary – the 'topic-neutral' or 'universal' vocabulary in all true theories. (See Appendix A.)

Definition 3 (Logical entailment) *Let X be a set of sentences of some language, say, $\{A_1, \ldots, A_n\}$, and let B be a sentence of the given language. Then, X logically entails B iff there's no logical possibility in which everything in X is true but B untrue.* (**Terminology**: *we sometimes abbreviate 'logical entailment' to* **logic**.)

Again, the space of *logical possibilities* is the widest space of possibilities; it's the space from which other entailment relations select relevant possibilities. (Again, there are logical possibilities in which all sorts of physically impossible things happen; however, the true theory of physics rules out such logical possibilities and treats them as irrelevant or, as in Section 1.1, *physically impossible*.)

Another special entailment relation (or, better, family of relations) is *predicate entailment*.

Definition 4 (Predicate-entailment relation) *Let P and Q be predicates in some language. Then, P predicate-entails ('p-entails' for short) Q iff there's no relevant possibility in which P is true of something but Q isn't true of the given something.*

Note that, in general, p-entailment and R-entailment (whether the R is logical entailment or otherwise) are intimately related but nonetheless distinct. Each is tied to a particular space of possibilities (viz., the space that the relation looks at for potential 'counterexamples'). On one hand, any p-entailment relation is (or inevitably delivers) an R-entailment relation. In particular, let the space of possibilities over which R-entailment is defined just be the space over which p-entailment is defined. In that case, predicate P p-entails Q just if Pc R-entails Qc, where c is any 'singular term' (a name or a refers-to-an-individual-object term). Moreover, provided that R-entailment is defined over a language with predicates (and any serious language has them), the converse direction also applies: Pc R-entails Qc iff P p-entails Q – at least where c is an arbitrary term.

1.3 Theories: Open and Closed

Truth-seeking theorists generally aim to advance not only the truth but the full truth; they aim to truly describe their target phenomenon and to do so as fully as possible. The resulting theory contains not only some scattered truths; the theory contains all *consequences* (or 'implications') of such truths, and all con-sequences of all such consequences of such truths, and so on. In this way, truth-seeking theorists, at least those after the full truth, have a twofold task constructing their target theories: first, they must put truths about the target phenomenon in their initial (say, 'seed') theory; second, they must 'close' the theory under an entailment (or consequence) relation for the theory.[1]

Definition 5 (Subset)   *Let X be any set of objects (e.g., any set of sentences, or apples, or tractors, or what have you). Then, Y is a* subset *of X iff everything in Y is also in X. (Moreover, Y is a* proper subset *of X iff Y is a subset of X but there's also some element of X which is not an element of Y.)*

Definition 6 (Set closed under entailment)   *Let X be any set of sentences from some language. Let R be an entailment (or consequence) relation for (or on) the given language. Then, X is* closed under R *(or R-closed) iff there's no subset of X that entails something that's not also in X. (In other words: X is closed under R iff there's no subset Y of X, and no sentence A of the given language, such that Y entails A according to R but A is not in the set X.)*

R-closed sets of sentences are so called because they are 'full' (or 'complete' or 'closed to the brim') with respect to the set's R-consequences (i.e., the con-sequences that, according to entailment relation R, follow from some subset of the set): if there's some claim entailed by something in the set, then the set, if closed under the given entailment relation, contains that claim. If the given set is true – that is, all sentences of the set are true – and if the set is closed under all appropriate entailment relations (more on this in Section 3), the set delivers not only the truth about its target domain of phenomena but the *full truth*, at least the full truth according to the given entailment relation.

In general, every language (and, hence, every language of every theory) has numerous entailment relations on it. (This will become clearer with examples, although we focus, for simplicity, on only two salient such relations, namely *logical* and *predicate* entailment relations – more on which in Section 3.) One can think of a language L having some associated (non-empty) set $\mathcal{R}$ of relevant entailment relations on it. From these ingredients come R-open theories and R-closed theories:

---

[1] Note well: the terms 'open set' and 'closed set' have very specific meanings in particular branches of mathematics (e.g., topology). The following use of such terms is *not* to be con-flated with any such commonly used terminology in maths; the terms in this discussion mean just what their definitions say – nothing more.

Definition 7 (*R*-Open Theory) *Let L be some language; let R contain entailment relations on L (i.e., all entailment relations over the same fragment of L); let R be one such entailment relation in R. An R-open theory in (or for or on) the language L is any set of L sentences that is not closed under R.*

Definition 8 (*R*-Closed Theory) *Let L be some language; let R contain entailment relations on L (i.e., all entailment relations over the same fragment of L); let R be one such entailment relation in R. An R-closed theory in (or for or on) the language L is any set of L sentences closed under R.*

Note that, with respect to Definition 8, a theory might be *R*-closed but not *R'*-closed, where *R* and *R'* are different entailment relations governing the same (fragment of) a language. This fact is not only relevant but important when it comes to the target topic of contradiction in christian theology (or, more explicitly, christian-theological theories).

1.4 Contradiction

Definition 9 (Formal Contradiction) *A sentence A is a* formal contradiction *iff it's of the form*

It is true that . . . and it is false that. . .

where both occurrences of '. . .' are replaced by one and the same sentence, the 'it is true that', 'it is false that' and the 'and' are logical *vocabulary.*[2]

Using logical notation (from Appendix A), a *formal contradiction* has the explicit form

$$\dagger A \wedge \neg A$$

where $\dagger$ is logic's (logically redundant) truth connective (sometimes 'logical nullation'); $\neg$ is logic's falsity connective (sometimes 'logical negation'); and $\wedge$ is logical conjunction. Given the logical redundancy of logic's truth connective, any formal contradiction has the implicit form

$$A \wedge \neg A.$$

Definition 10 (Contradiction) *A sentence A is a* contradiction *in a theory iff A entails, according to the theory's relevant entailment relation, a formal contradiction.*

---

[2] See Appendix A for logical vocabulary.

Definition 11 (Contradictory)   *A sentence A is* contradictory *in a theory iff A entails, according to the theory's relevant entailment relation, a contradiction. A set X of sentences is contradictory (in a theory) iff X entails a contradiction (in said theory).*

2 The Threat of Contradiction

The principal threat of contradiction for a would-be true theory is 'triviality', which may be understood via so-called trivial theories.

2.1 Trivial Theories

Triviality is the uncontroversial paradigm of an absurd theory:

Definition 12 (Trivial Theory)   *Let L be some language. Then, $T^\perp$ (pronounced 'T-bottom') is the* trivial theory *in L iff $T^\perp$ contains all L sentences (i.e., all sentences in the language are true according to $T^\perp$).*

There's a general fact concerning *some* entailment relations and any would-be true (closed) theory. The target fact is straightforward given the idea of a *logically explosive* or *logically exclusive* entailment relation:

Definition 13 (Logically Explosive/Exclusive Entailment)   *Let R be an entailment relation over language L, and let A and B be L sentences. Finally, let ¬ and ∧ be logical negation and logical conjunction (i.e., logical 'and'), so that, for example, ¬A is the logical negation of A, and A ∧ B is the logical conjunction of A and B. Then, R is* logically explosive *(equivalently,* logically exclusive*) iff arbitrary A ∧ ¬A R-entails arbitrary B.*[3]

The terminology reflects the fact that, according to any such entailment relation R, one cannot have both A and its logical negation $\neg A$ in a theory without having *all* sentences of the language in the R-closure of that theory; the theory 'explodes' into the trivial one for the language in the presence of contradiction. This, in the end, is the target general fact:

Fact 1 (Exploding Theories into Triviality)   *Let R be a logically explosive entailment relation. Let T be a theory closed under R. Let the language of T*

---

[3]   More generally, the definition is that $\{A, \neg A\}$ R-entails arbitrary B iff R is logically explosive/exclusive; however, for present purposes, wherein all canvassed accounts of logical conjunction have various features, the given general account is equivalent to the otherwise more limited one. We stick with the latter because it simplifies discussion of contradiction.

contain all logical vocabulary. Then, T contains a formal contradiction iff the R-closure of T is $T^{\perp}$, the trivial theory in T's language.

2.2 Theology, Contradiction, and Triviality

Given Fact 1 (in Section 2.1), it's clear that any would-be true theology is either

- *the trivial theology* (for the given language) *or*
- contains no contradictions *or*
- is not closed under a logically explosive entailment relation.

The same applies to any would-be true theory (of anything), but christian theism is the target topic.[4]

3 Outline of Target Abstract Responses in General

For present purposes, we simplify discussion by assuming that contradictions follow, if at all, from axioms in a given theory, where *axioms* are simply core truths of the theory – not in any way necessarily 'self-evident' or the like. In the case of theological theories, axioms often take the form of central doctrines. (Examples are given below.)

---

[4] The claim is in fact true only given our simplifying assumption that theology's predicate-entailment relation does not treat standard axioms (e.g., the humanity and divinity of Christ; the trinitarian identity of Father, Son, Spirit; etc.) as 'explosive' in the following sense.

Definition 14 (*R*-explosive sentence) *Let A and B be sentences in language L. Let R be a relevant entailment relation for theory T. A is R-explosive iff A R-entails B for all B in L (where 'A R-entails B' just means that A entails B according to entailment relation R).*

Definition 15 (*R*-explosive set of sentences) *Let X be a set of sentences in language L, and A any sentence in L. Let R be a relevant entailment relation for theory T. X is R-explosive iff X R-entails A for all A in L (where 'X R-entails A' just means that X entails A according to entailment relation R).*

Given all of this, the true general claim is that, given Fact 1, any would-be true theology is either

- *the trivial theology* (for the given language) *or*
- contains no contradictions *or*
- is not closed under a logically explosive entailment relation *or*
- either contains no *R*-explosive sentences or is not *R*-closed.

In the face of derived contradiction, one response is to reject one or more of the initial axioms. For our purposes – focussing on christian theological theory – we do not discuss that approach. Our aim is to discuss responses that preserve the basic axioms (i.e., preserve central doctrines, as illustrated in subsequent sections).[5]

Suppose that a contradiction is derived from given axioms of a given theory (e.g., on our focus, a theology). For present purposes, there are basically three avenues of response, each with different avenues of implementation.[6]

- *Partial Theology.* Theology is not closed under otherwise governing entailment relations (e.g., logical or the relevant predicate-entailment relations); it is R-open with respect to at least one salient, relevant entailment relation R. (Examples in subsequent sections.) Accordingly, the would-be entailment of apparent contradiction need be no threat *to the given theory* so long as the theory omits relevant entailments or consequences that deliver the contradiction.

- *Robust Theology (1).* *Closed under standard logic and non-standard predicate entailment.* Theology is closed under both (theological) predicate entailment and logical entailment, where logical entailment is (logically) explosive but theological predicate entailment, contrary to the standard relation, does not deliver the given contradiction. Hence, the apparent contradiction is merely apparent.

- *Robust Theology (2).* *Closed under non-standard logic and standard predicate entailment.* Theology is closed under both (theological) predicate entailment and logical entailment, where theological predicate entailment delivers the given contradiction but logical entailment is *not* (logically) explosive. Hence, the principal threat from the theory's contradiction(s) is merely apparent.

Each of the avenues of response enjoys different avenues of implementation. For present purposes, at most one route towards implementing given responses is canvassed, letting that route be a representative (though, to repeat, the given representatives neither exhaust the options nor necessarily realize historically occupied responses).

---

[5] Rejecting the axioms is tantamount to rejecting the given theory/theology. This is what so-called theological heresies do: reject the standard theory by rejecting one or more axioms. Our aim in this Element is only to cover options for retention of the axioms as far as possible.

[6] There are other combinatorial options but we focus only on the following three salient ones.

TWO PRINCIPAL EXAMPLES

4 One Central Example: Incarnation

In what follows, the term 'axiom' is not intended to convey any epistemic status (e.g., 'self-evident' or 'obvious' or what have you); the term is used simply to flag that, at least in the standard christian theology (e.g., at least up through the 451 CE Council of Chalcedon), these claims are taken to be fundamental – even partly definitive – of the target phenomenon. Epistemic grounds for such claims is a different issue, one on which this discussion remains neutral (beyond noting that the grounds usually involve revelation as recorded in christian scriptural records and in the catholic christian church).

1. Christ is divine.
   Source: theological axiom.
2. Christ is human.
   Source: theological axiom.
3. Christ is omniscient.
   Source: from (1) by theology's *predicate-entailment* relation.
4. Christ is non-omniscient.
   Source: from (2) by theology's *predicate-entailment* relation.[7]
5. It's false that Christ is omniscient.
   Source: (4) by theology's *predicate-entailment* relation.
6. Christ is omniscient and it's false that Christ is omniscient.
   Source: from (3)–(5) by *logical* entailment.

5 Partial Theology: Responses to the Incarnation

For simplicity, focus exclusively on the apparent contradiction in Section 4. One family of responses to the apparent contradiction is to pursue a true theology but not the full truth. There are other responses (viz., so-called QUA or 'reduplicative' responses) that try to retain the axioms by claiming either that they're equivocal or that they are implicitly other than what is explicit – not just 'Christ is ignorant' but rather 'Christ-qua-human is ignorant' or etc. (Cross, 2011; Senor, 2002). We do not discuss such approaches; rather, we discuss

---

[7] For any who think that *being human* does not entail *being ignorant* (i.e., ignorant of at least some things), the claim is also standardly supported via scriptural revelation in christian theology (e.g., Mark 13:32). For ease of exposition, claim (5) in the given derivation is taken to follow from claim (2) via standard meanings of 'human' and 'non-omniscient'. (Some might say that the meaning of 'human' doesn't entail – necessitate – non-omniscience; however, the standard christian tradition is in tension with the genuine possibility that humans are completely on par with the omniscient God, and this is one of many reasons that the target apparent contradiction involved in the incarnation doctrine is so common.)

just those options that keep the axioms as they are.[8] Of course, inasmuch as, according to the standard christian theology, divine reality remains mysterious in some respects to any but divine beings, 'the full truth' in this context just means *as full as possible*. That the full truth is beyond the capacities of non-divine theorists is entirely compatible with a theology that records the full truth as far as possible within the bounds of possibility open to non-divine beings.

Partial theology, per Definition 7, is simply theology that aims only at *R*-open theories, theologies – theories of the divine – that are not closed under one or more of the otherwise salient 'governing' entailment relations *R*. For present purposes, there are two salient entailment relations involved in the target contradiction (see Section 4): logical entailment and the standard predicate-entailment relation, where the latter validates the entailments marked 'predicate entailment' in the guiding example. A relevant open theology is closed under at most one of the two said entailment relations.

Open theology, as herein discussed, comes in three basic approaches, depending on the entailment relations in play. The following three approaches do not exhaust the combinatorial possibilities; they rather represent the options that are most natural were one to pursue partial theology in response to contradiction. (If one's theology were closed under a non-standard account of logical entailment, especially one, as in Section 6.3, that accommodates contradictions, the motivation for partial theology may be diminished.)

5.1 Closed Under No Entailment At All

This is just a set of claims without their respective consequences (or, at least, without all of the consequences). In particular, a natural implementation of the *closed-under-none* approach takes the theological theory to contain *just* the axioms (1) and (2) of Section 4 and none of the other claims that *otherwise* follow from (1) and (2) by the salient entailment relations otherwise governing the full truth of Christ.

5.1.1 Historical Examples

No historical examples of such an explicitly *closed-under-none* approach are known. Coakley (2002) argues that the relevant ecumenical councils – especially up through Chalcedon 451 – lay down apparent contradiction (or 'paradox') without explicitly cashing out the consequences; however, it is

---

[8] Of course, some of the given responses that we do not discuss are framed as uncovering the implicit forms of the 'axioms as they are', but we treat such responses more as alternative semantics (especially of singular terms but perhaps also predicates or even the exemplification relation) rather than attending to salient entailment relations.

unclear whether, even on Coakley's account of the matter, the theology is supposed to remain unclosed with respect to salient entailment relations.[9]

5.1.2 Comment

There are conspicuous problems with the *closed-under-none* account. For just one, the theory entails contradiction but the theory avoids it by simply ignoring the given entailments. The theory *is* contradictory, in the sense of truly entailing contradiction; it just doesn't contain its contradictions because it avoids facing its own consequences, so to speak. The problem is that such an approach, shy of supplemental argument for the flee from entailment, is clearly not in a truth-seeking enterprise. Instead of a 'faith-seeking understanding' strategy, the strategy is very much a 'faith hiding from truth' strategy.

5.2 Standard Logical but No Predicate Entailment

This is the partial-theology route that is subject to logical entailment but not to any predicate-entailment relation; it results in a theology closed under standard (so-called classical) logic but not under any predicate-entailment relation.

This approach allows would-be contradictory claims without the contradictions, such as (1) and (2) without (3)–(5), or even (3) and (4) without (5). The strategy reflects the standard predicate-entailment relation and the standard 'classical' account of logical entailment; however, the true theology is only closed under logical entailment, not under the given predicate-entailment relation. Accordingly, the theological theory can contain genuinely contradictory claims in the sense that, *were the theory closed under the standard predicate-entailment relation*, the theory would 'logically explode' into the trivial theology – that is, the theology that contains all sentences in the language of the theory. But so long as at least some of the predicate consequences are left out of the theory – for example, claim (5) in the given derivation – the theology avoids the threat of contradiction that is otherwise a very live threat given that the theology is closed under classical-logic entailment. (According to the classical-logic account of logical entailment, an arbitrary contradiction $A \wedge \neg A$ logically entails *all* sentences whatsoever in the language, and so the theory, if closed under classical logic, collapses into the trivial theology. In short, the classical-logic account is explosive, per Definition 13, with respect to arbitrary contradictions.)

---

[9] See too McCall (2015, 2021) for similar discussion.

5.2.1 Historical Precedent

There is no clear case of closing only under the classical-logic entailment relation but not under any predicate-entailment relation. Once again, the discussion by Coakley (2002) suggests that perhaps some 'apophatic' traditions are understood along these lines, where 'apophatic' traditions are ones wherein, in some sense (alas, to our knowledge, left imprecise), divine reality is truly or falsely described *only negatively* (in some sense).[10]

On the other hand, many of the conciliar texts (i.e., documents from 'stamped' ecumenical councils) only explicitly give the claims that, if closed under the standard predicate-entailment relation, entail the contradictions (e.g., that Christ is mutable/changeable and immutable/unchangeable). Accordingly, one way of thinking about some of the given theological texts in many target ecumenical councils is that they're advancing an open theological theory of just the running variety: closed (say) under logical entailment (where logical entailment is taken to be at least logically explosive with respect to contradiction) but not under any relevant predicate-entailment relation.

5.2.2 Comment

The prima facie problem with this approach is very similar to that of the *closed-under-none* approach (per Section 5.1), but one can think of it as a dilemma. Either the theologian knows the relevant meanings of predicates (or at least sufficiently much of them) or not. Suppose that the theorist (the theologian) knows the predicate-entailment relation governing the meanings of target terms (e.g., 'divine', 'human', etc.). The theorist sees that axioms (1) and (2) directly (predicate-) entail (3)–(5), respectively; however, because the theology is closed under a logically explosive entailment relation (viz., the classical-logic relation), the theorist simply dams the otherwise flood of predicate entailments by refusing to close the theory under said predicate entailment. The problem with this 'horn' is that the theologian is thereby advancing a theory known to be contradictory – because it does entail contradiction according to the relevant predicate-entailment relation – but in fact not contradictory because its consequences are blocked from being in the theory. Suppose, on the other hand, that the theorist doesn't know the relevant meanings (or sufficiently much of them). The problem with this 'horn' is that the theologian is knowingly advancing axioms the relevant meanings of which are unknown.

---

[10] Note well: we are not suggesting that Coakley asserts any claim to the effect that some apophatic traditions are best understood as advancing a theology closed under classical-logic entailment but not under standard predicate entailment. Rather, Coakley's discussion opens up this possibility with respect to historical tradition.

5.3 Standard Predicate Entailment Only

This is the partial-theology route that is subject to the standard predicate-entailment relation but not to logical entailment; it results in an open theology closed under standard predicate entailment but not under logical entailment.

This approach validates the derivation of claims (3)–(5) but not claim (6), since only (3)–(5) are consequences of the predicate-entailment relation under which the theology is closed; (6) is a logical consequence of claims in the given theology but the theology, on this open-theology approach, is not closed under logical entailment.

5.3.1 Historical Precedent

Historical precedent is unclear. (The unclarity, as in the other options above, arises more from silence about the exact entailment relations involved than a clear absence of theorists falling under the given approach.) But there are theologians whose work may – *not at all to hereby say 'clearly do'* – fall into the running approach, in particular theologians such as Dahms (1978), possibly Luther (see Lehmann 1971), and perhaps also 'paradoxical theologians' such as Kierkegaard. We leave scholars of such theorists to decide.

5.3.2 Comment

The prima facie problem with this approach is that while the theology avoids the explicit formal contradiction in (6), the theory is nonetheless logically contradictory in the sense that it *logically* entails the trivial theology – the theology in which all claims in the language of theology are true. The theory itself avoids its triviality by blocking logical consequences from being in the theology. This may go hand in hand with a rejection of the truth-seeking aims of theology, but such a rejection requires supplemental argument. Pending successful such argument, the approach carries an appearance of irresponsibility with respect to truth – similar to that of foregoing approaches to partial theology.

6 Robust Theology: Responses to the Incarnation

Partial theology, as discussed in Section 3, purports to seek truth but not the whole truth. *Robust theology*, in contrast with partial theology, aims at the full truth (i.e., as full as possible); it results in a theological theory that is closed under both logical entailment and predicate entailment. The various avenues towards robust theology differ on their accounts of logical and predicate entailment, where these (together or separately) may deviate from the standard accounts.

6.1 Standard Logical and Standard Predicate Entailment

A robust theology is closed under both of the salient entailment relations, namely logical and predicate entailment relations. The robust theology closed under both of the *standard* entailment relations is just the trivial theology. After all, the standard relations validate the target derivation in Section 4, from which the standard (so-called classical-logic) relation immediately results in trivial theology.

6.1.1 Historical Precedent

Nobody has explicitly (if at all) pursued this form of robust theology – that is, a trivial theology.

6.1.2 Comment

And nobody should. The only 'virtue' of the given approach is that it necessarily delivers all truths of divine reality, and does so in a simple way. If you throw *all* sentences of the language of a theory (theological or otherwise) into the theory then you're guaranteed to get all truths of the target phenomenon. The downside, of course, is that you equally inexorably get all untruths expressible in the language of the theory.

6.2 Standard Logical but Non-standard Predicate Entailment

This is the robust-theology route that is subject to the standard logical-entailment relation (i.e., so-called classical-logic entailment) but to some non-standard predicate-entailment relation or other; it results in a theology closed under standard logic but closed under a non-standard predicate-entailment relation.

6.2.1 Historical Precedent

The standard-logic but non-standard-predicate response is common. For historical sources and varieties of response, see the Element by Pawl (2020).

For but one example, recent works by Cross (2011) and Pawl (2016, 2019) illustrate different implementations of the standard-logical but nonstandard-predicate approach. For simplicity, what follows is just one simple way in which such an approach might go; the following is not the actual theory of any theologian (though what follows has similarities to some historically realized theologies).

Let logical entailment be per the classical-logic account. Given the derivation in Section 4, the *standard* predicate-entailment relation demands the following:[11]

- *x* is *omniscient* iff it's true that *x* knows all relevant truths.[12]
- *x* is *non-omniscient* iff it's false that *x* knows all relevant truths.

So goes (a small but relevant fragment of) the *standard* predicate-entailment relation. That's the predicate-entailment relation behind the sample derivation in Section 4. On the current non-standard predicate-entailment response to the contradiction, some other predicate-entailment relation governs the true theology. In particular, the relevant axioms of the theory do not involve 'omniscient' and 'non-omniscient' per above; they rather involve '⋆-omniscient' and '⋆-non-omniscient', where these are governed by a predicate-entailment relation that demands only the following:

- *x* is *⋆-omniscient* iff *some part of x* is omniscient.
- *x* is *⋆-non-omniscient* iff *some part of x* is non-omniscient.

While the predicate-entailment relation for starred predicates is not the standard one for relevant unstarred predicates, the relation affords room to avoid target contradictions while nonetheless advancing a robust – entirely closed – theology. 'Affords room' is not 'guarantees'. Details, of course, matter. On this approach, axioms (1) and (2), from Section 4, are either themselves starred or governed only by the non-standard predicate-entailment relation: (1) and (2), according to the target approach, jointly entail at most the starred variations of (3) and (4), namely

- Christ is ⋆-omniscient.
- Christ is ⋆-non-omniscient.

Provided that the theology is bolstered by some suitable metaphysics (and, in particular, so-called mereology), wherein Christ can have an 'omniscient part' and a 'non-omniscient part', the apparent contradiction in the target derivation in Section 4 may be avoided. Presumably, it's easy enough to have non-omniscient parts if one is human; having an omniscient *part* may be more difficult even if one is divine (especially if divinity involves 'simplicity'

---

[11] What follows is put in simple (so-called) biconditional form rather than forms that lay out an actual predicate-entailment relation. This is entirely for simplicity.

[12] Note: the scope of 'all relevant truths' is left to the reader, as this is orthogonal to the approach being illustrated.

in the sense of being without parts). Still, the general approach towards a non-standard predicate-entailment relation is sufficiently clear for present purposes.

6.2.2 Comment

One potential problem with the given non-standard predicate-entailment approach is notable. At least in the crude form illustrated in Section 6.2.1, the given approach appears to shift the subject from *Christ's* being omniscient and non-omniscient to *some part that is not Christ* being omniscient and non-omniscient. (Strictly, to avoid the contradiction, which, per the standard logical entailment relation, is explosive with respect to contradiction, only one of 'Christ is omniscient' and 'Christ is non-omniscient' needs to shift to some part that is not Christ.) The original axioms appeared to be speaking of *Christ's* divinity and humanity; however, at least one of those axioms is ultimately speaking of something other than Christ – some *part* which is not Christ – at least on the given strategy above.

Another potential problem for such accounts points to would-be reasons for firmly accepting the standard account of logical entailment (viz., the so-called classical account). There is little doubt that the standard account gets its historical target correct: namely, the entailment behaviour of logical vocabulary in (standard) true mathematical theories. But why think that the entailment behaviour of logical vocabulary in true *mathematical* theories is the entailment behaviour of logical vocabulary in *all* true theories – theology included? There is no strong argument for thinking as much. Why, then, cling to the standard account of logical entailment and reject the standard entailment relations governing theological predicates? The potential problem with doing so is that the strategy appears to be as firm as the reasons for sticking to the standard story about logical entailment – reasons that, as above, are dubious at best.

6.2.3 Further Comment on Epistemic-Mystery Responses

One might wonder wherein so-called epistemic-mystery accounts of apparent contradiction fit, such as that of Anderson (2007), which is the most worked-out such account. At least on said account, *both* the standard (so-called classical) account of logical entailment *and* the standard predicate-entailment relation are supposed to be in play. Anderson's given work argues that the theory is nonetheless rational to hold. The question is: what is the theory? In the end, the epistemic-mystery account – as advanced in its clearest form (viz., Anderson's) – avoids the trivial theology by endorsing a non-standard predicate-entailment relation. The trouble, according to the epistemic-mystery account, is that there's mystery as to what the non-standard predicate-entailment relation happens to be. We leave comparison of this sort of standard-logic but non-standard-predicate-entailment account with relevant non-epistemic-mystery cousins (such as in Section 6.2.1) to the reader.

6.3 Standard Predicate but Non-standard Logical Entailment

The details of this approach turn on the sort of non-standard logical-entailment relation involved. For present purposes, the approach is illustrated via a so-called subclassical account of logic, namely the so-called FDE account (so called for 'first-degree entailment').[13]

Here, the standard predicate-entailment relation governing theology is active (so to speak). The derivation from axioms (1) and (2) down to (5) is validated on the current approach, *as is the ultimate derivation of contradiction* at (6).[14] What is *not* validated is the step *from* (6) to the trivial theology. Details aside (see Appendix A), a suitable non-standard account of logical entailment is one that does not validate the would-be derivation of *all sentences* in the language from *an* arbitrary contradiction.

On the current approach (of which there can be many implementations), the true theology is contradictory; it contains contradictions, such as, for example, (6) in Section 4. On such an approach, the space of logical possibilities allows for 'true contradictions' (i.e., gluts of truth and falsity) without thereby demanding the actuality of them.[15]

6.3.1 Historical Precedent

The most explicit historical precedent of such an approach is advanced by Beall (2021, 2023), though initially puzzling and apparently contradictory remarks by a host of theological thinkers (e.g., Tertullian, Leo's Tome, Luther, Ratzinger, Barth, and perhaps various mystics) suggest the target approach even if the remarks were at most implicit.[16]

---

[13] Sufficient details are given in Appendix A.

[14] One could underwrite theology with a so-called non-adjunctive account of logical entailment that would thereby invalidate the step from (3) and (5) to (6); however, for illustration, we discuss only accounts of logical entailment that validate the given step.

[15] But see Restall (1997) for issues around possibility and actuality arising along some directions of such theories. (Worth noting is that Restall's given derivation is invalid in the current, so-called FDE context.)

[16] Cotnoir (2018) deserves credit for explicitly advocating the exploration of contradictory theology, even if he doesn't – in the given work – advocate a particular theological theory.

6.3.2 Comment

While some might consider the contradictory approach to be problematic in virtue of contradiction alone, a position that would require argument,[17] a different potential problem is notable. The problem resides in 'full and explicit belief' of such central theological contradictions. How, for example, does one *fully and saliently – all at once in 'the mind's eye'* – believe such allegedly contradictory truths such as, for but exactly one example, (6)? It's one thing to believe all at once (3). It's one thing to believe all at once (4). But (6)? The worry is that, on the given contradictory approach, the very theology – the given contradictory theory taken to truly describe divine reality – is not fully believable. At least prima facie this is a potential problem, though perhaps it is entwined with the essential mysteries of divine reality. Discussion is left for any would-be contradictory theology.

7 Another Central Example: Trinity

Another central example is the other distinctively christian apparent contradiction, namely the trinity, which, together with the incarnation, forms a distinctive core of apparent christian contradictory doctrine. An example of apparent trinitarian contradiction is as follows.

1. Father is God and Son is God and Spirit is God.
   Source: theological axiom.
2. It's false that Father is Son and false that Son is Spirit and false that Spirit is Father.
   Source: theological axiom.
3. *Entailment fact:* (1) entails that Father is Son and Son is Spirit and Spirit is Father.
   Source: predicate entailment concerning 'identity', specifically, transitivity of identity.
4. It's true that Father is Son and true that Son is Spirit and true that Spirit is Father.
   Source: (1) and (3).
5. It's true and false that Father is Son and Son is Spirit and Spirit is Father.[18]
   Source: logical entailment from (2) and (4).

---

[17] The work of early pioneers outside of theology – such as, but not limited to, Asenjo (1966), Priest (2006), Mortensen (1995), and Routley and Meyer (1976) – have helped to make plain that the logical possibility of true and *non-trivial* contradictory theories in general is viable, though details always matter.

[18] We use *It's true and false that* as shorthand for the explicit contradiction.

8 Partial Theology: Responses to the Trinity

Apparent contradictions arising from core christian axioms (1) and (2) have enjoyed a lot – a lot, a lot – of attention since, at the very least, 451 CE and the Council of Chalcedon. The fierce attention continues to this day (at least at the time of this writing, in 2022). Since this is not an Element on the trinity (or the incarnation, or any of the many omni-god issues), we strip the discussion to very elemental levels to illustrate the general (and abstract) pattern of entailment-relation responses.

One issue from the start: a common response is to reject the prima facie appearance of an identity relation in the core 'identity' axioms (1) and (2), where (2), prima facie, consists of logically negated identity sentences (e.g., *it's false that Father is Son*, etc.). Instead, the 'is' in such axioms is taken to be predicative, part of the spelling of some predicate (e.g., not 'Father is identical to God' but rather 'Father is god-ish' or 'Father is divine' or 'Father exemplifies god-ness' or the like). Any such response may be seen either as a rejection of the original axioms (taken to be identity axioms) or a weakening of the predicate-entailment relation governing such axioms – at least to the extent that the transitivity entailment fact is no longer involved.

For our purposes (which, again, do not involve a discussion of either the target problems or their historical treatments), we focus only on (1) and (2) as *identity* axioms – or logically negated identity axioms. For discussion of the many (many) different issues revolving around apparent trinitarian contradiction, see Coakley (2013); Crisp and Sanders (2014); Hasker (2013); McCall (2010); McCall and Rea (2009); Rea (2009).

** *An observation.* What makes apparent trinitarian – and also incarnation-related – contradiction prima facie more striking than the other examples (e.g., omni-property contradictions, discussed in subsequent sections) is that the contradiction appears to be conspicuous *in the very axioms of standard/orthodox theology.* In particular, just as with the axioms concerning the 'full divinity' and 'full humanity' of Christ (which is enough for the standard predicate-entailment relations to deliver the contradiction), so too – perhaps even more so – with the trinitarian identity axioms. These axioms, perhaps unlike 'omnipotence' or the like, are core doctrines – a sort of *officially stamped axiomatic status* – concerning the target phenomena. Given that their flat-footed, prima facie standard implications deliver contradiction, the contradictions concerning the trinity and incarnation often appear to be of more critical importance than some of the other examples. To what extent this observation is either important or fruitful is left to the reader. *End observation.* **

8.1 Closed under No Entailment At All

As with other examples, the closed-under-none is basically a free-for-all, do-whatever-you-wish, no-consequences sort of response to contradiction. In particular, since not closed under any entailment relation, the theory can contain only axioms (1) and (2) without any of (4)–(5) in the theory. Likewise, since not closed under any entailment relation, the theory can contain only (1), (2), and (4) or only (1), (2), and (5) in the theory.[19] For that matter, being entirely unconstrained by its would-be consequences, the theology can contain *all* of (1), (2), (4), and (5) without in any way reducing to the trivial theology (i.e., the theology that contains all sentences in the language of the theology). Any such closed-under-none theology might be the absolute paradigm of *non*-systematic theology.

8.1.1 Historical Examples

We know of no historical examples.

8.1.2 Comment

The situation here is the same, mutatis mutandis, with the incarnation contradiction in Section 5.1.

8.2 Standard Logic but No Predicate Entailment

On this approach, core identity axioms (1) and (2) are in the theory but, since not closed under standard (or any) predicate-entailment relation, the theology is not bound by background fact (3) concerning the (standard) implications of 'identity'. Accordingly, the theory need not contain (4), and so, even though it's closed under standard (so-called classical) logical entailment, the theology needn't contain the contradiction (5).[20]

8.2.1 Historical Precedent

We know of no historical precedent.

8.2.2 Comment

The closed-only-under-logic approach, on the surface, appears to be more systematic and truth-seeking than the closed-under-none approach, but refusing

---

[19] As throughout this Element, we are not discussing responses that jettison the core axioms; hence, we only discuss theologies that contain at least (1) and (2).

[20] And it can't either, since otherwise, being closed under standard logical entailment, the theology would be reduced to the trivial theology if it contained either (4) or (5).

to hold a would-be truth-seeking theory to its full consequences ultimately appears to be unsystematic. Moreover, for what symmetry is worth, the approach is not symmetric in the way that the closed-under-none approach is symmetric. (Why *that* entailment relation rather than *that* one?) Symmetry favours either a *closed-under-both* or a *closed-under-neither* approach.

8.3 Standard Predicate Entailment Only

This option closes under standard predicate entailment but not under standard (or any other would-be) logical entailment. Since axioms (1) and (2) are fixed, and they contain only an identity predicate as the central predicate, (4) is in the theory given background entailment fact (3) and (1) together. Not being closed under standard (or any) logical entailment, (5) needn't be in the theory. Accordingly, on the standard-predicate-only approach to the target contradiction (5), the theology contains all of (1), (2), and (4), but not (5).

8.3.1 Historical Precedent

We know of no historical precedent that explicitly spells out the resulting theory; however, as in other examples, Dahms (1978), even though not clearly expressed, is clear precedent of the running approach.

8.3.2 Comment

The comment in Section 8.2.2, mutatis mutandis, applies in this case too.

9 Robust Theology: Responses to the Trinity

Robust theology, unlike open theology, takes seriously that theology seeks not only the truth but also the full truth, including all consequences of whatever claims are in the theory.[21] The options, as throughout the examples, require closing under both logical entailment and predicate entailment; the differences among approaches turn on differences in the entailment relations involved.

9.1 Standard Logic and Standard Predicate Entailment

As with other examples, the standard-logic and standard-predicate response results in the trivial theology. Standard logical entailment governs only the 'adjunction' from (2) and (4) to the contradiction (5) – and then, being the

---

[21] As said elsewhere, the aim is not in any way incompatible with explicit epistemic bounds on theorists to reach the full truth of divine reality. Since it is unclear where exactly the limitations hit the ground, the responsible task is to seek the full truth and see where one ends.

standard (so-called classical) logical-entailment relation, from (5) to the trivial theology. Were (4) not part of the theory, the contradiction wouldn't (need to) be in the theory; however, (4) is in the theory given closure under standard predicate entailment, which governs the central predicate (viz., identity) involved in axioms (1) and (2).

9.1.1 Historical Examples

There are none.

9.1.2 Comment

Nor should there be.

9.2 Standard Logic but Non-standard Predicate Entailment

This response, as with other examples, is by far the dominant one. The key feature of this response, regardless of the details of the many various implementations, is a rejection of the lone predicate-entailment fact in the background, namely (3). Being a robust theology (and, so, closed under both logical and predicate entailment relations), some other predicate-entailment is invoked. While there are many options, one condition is clear: namely, that the entailment relation invalidates transitivity of the target identity relation (i.e., that the given identity predicate is not transitive according to said predicate-entailment relation).[22]

9.2.1 Historical Precedent

Though implemented along very different lines (and, in some cases, not treating axioms as *identity* axioms as we are assuming for simplicity), most contemporary responses to trinitarian contradiction fall under this response. See Hasker (2013); McCall (2010); McCall and Rea (2009); Rea (2009); and van Inwagen (1988, 1994) for a variety of examples.

---

[22] See Section 8 for a reminder of the complexity of responses to trinitarian contradiction and also the simplifying assumptions we are making for present purposes. One complexity worth highlighting here is that so-called relative-identity responses – wherein there's no unique identity predicate involved in all target axioms but rather many different ones (all governed by some predicate-entailment relation) – are often said to be not only transitive but also symmetric and reflexive (and, thus, so-called equivalence relations). This makes sense only if the *names* (generally, *singular terms*) in the given axioms – and the language of theology, generally – have a very non-standard semantics. Unfortunately, there are few details of the requisite semantics, though some suggestions towards potential accounts. For details on so-called relative-identity responses, see, among others, the work by Geach (1980); Jedwab (2015); Martinich (1978, 1979); Rea (2003), as well as references therein, and also Beall (2023).

9.2.2 Comment

A curiosity of the common standard-logic but non-standard-predicate response is that the would-be critical identity relation (or, in other directions, family of identity relations) remains largely undefined. For a robust-theological response, this situation is less than ideal. Normally, one defines an identity relation along 'leibnizian' lines utilizing some conditional → (and forming a biconditional ↔ via logical conjunction) and the 'leibnizian-schema' recipe to the effect that objects x and y stand in the identity relation just when all instances of the schema $\varphi(x) \leftrightarrow \varphi(y)$ are true, for all relevant predicates φ in the language of the theory. While the standard leibnizian-recipe approach towards defining identity relations is not required by theology, *some* precise definition is required, one that makes plain the relevant resulting predicate-entailment behaviour of the defined predicate in the target axioms.[23]

9.3 Standard Predicate but Non-standard Logical Entailment

This response begins, in the background, by acknowledging that there's no strong argument for the standard account of logical entailment, and that there's good reason to accept a weaker account. (As throughout, for present purposes we assume FDE per Appendix A, though implementations of the current response can take different directions from FDE.) But notice: even with a weaker-than-classical relation of logical entailment, sentence (4) is still stuck in the theory if the predicate-entailment relation is standard. Inasmuch as (4) is as 'explosive' in standard (christian) theology as the logical negation of 'God is omnibenevolent' (i.e., both sentences are in the theology only if the theology is the trivial theology),[24] such a non-standard logical-entailment relation does no work whatsoever in dealing with the given contradiction (5). Logic, on this approach, won't take the theology to the trivial theology; however, on the assumption that (4) itself is 'explosive' in said ways, the theology's extra-logical entailment relation (or, to simplify, the target predicate-entailment relation) takes the theory to the trivial one.

---

[23] We note that, so far as we see, even leaders in the relative-identity responses come up short of satisfying said task, including Hasker (2013); McCall (2010); McCall and Rea (2009); Rea (2009); and van Inwagen (1988, 1994). Further discussion is given by Beall (2021).

[24] Another way to think of this: there's no *theological possibility* – that is, no possibility recognized by the entailment relation underwriting the theology – in which either (4) or 'It's false that God is omnibenevolent' is true. If there's no such possibility, then such sentences being true according to the theory thereby entail the trivial theory, in the same way that, *according to the classical-logic relation*, there is no possibility in which a contradiction is true, and so any theory that contains a contradiction and is underwritten by (closed under) classical logic is reduced to the trivial theory.

What all readers are thinking is that the would-be standard-predicate and non-standard-logic approach – *or at least one flavour of it* – can and should reject that (4) alone predicate-entails the trivial theory. True. The end result, on this approach, is a theology that contains all of (1), (2), (4), and (5) without thereby being the trivial theology.

What remains is the important fact that an alternative flavour of the current approach (i.e., standard predicate but non-standard logical entailment) is not viable if (4) itself is explosive according to the theology's predicate-entailment relation. (Section 9.3.2 discusses a variation in which non-standard-logical and non-standard-predicate entailment relations are involved.)

9.3.1 Historical Precedent

To our knowledge, there is no historical precedent for the given approaches (as described); however, there is a variation described in Section 9.3.2.

9.3.2 Comment

The viability of a standard-predicate but non-standard-logic approach, as in Section 9.3, is unclear, turning on the status of (4). Any glut-theoretic response to contradiction is one in which some axioms or their implications are gluts (i.e., both true according to the theory and false according to the theory); however, some claims in the theory might be *just true according to the theory* or *just false according to the theory* – and 'necessarily so' in the sense that the relevant entailment relation for the theory recognizes no possibility (beyond, perhaps, just the trivial possibility) in which such sentences are true. Which sentences are gluts and which are just true or the like is not something that has a general solution procedure; it's a case-by-case matter. But, for present purposes, suppose that (4) is explosive in the true theology.

A historical (though very recent) variant of – or mild deviation from – the standard-predicate and non-standard-logic approach to trinitarian contradiction is one that is *non-standard for both* entailment relations. In particular, the identity predicate involved in trinitarian axioms is not transitive; hence, the background (standard) predicate-entailment fact (3) does not govern the theory. Moreover, logical entailment, on this approach, is also non-standard – and, again, for present purposes, FDE (see Appendix A). This is the avenue advanced by Beall (2023).[25] The prima facie advantage of this approach over other non-standard-predicate (but standard-logic) approaches is that there's a

---

[25] Beall (2023) presents a general framework for identity relations. One of many identity relations that falls out of said general framework is explored in a metaphysical direction under the guise of 'dialetheism' by Priest (2014).

simple, precise, *leibnizian-recipe* definition of the identity relation in (1) and (2), one that easily explains the *non-transitivity* (and likewise failure of standard substitution principles) of the relation. Details are given in said work, but the gist is that the identity relation is defined in the usual leibnizian-recipe way but uses logic's biconditional per FDE (versus the biconditional per so-called classical logic). Since said biconditional is itself nontransitive in any theory (such as theology) wherein the possibility of contradictions is recognized (by the given predicate-entailment relation), the resulting identity relation is nontransitive. In the particular theory by Beall (2023), (1) is a glut according to the theory (i.e., both true according to the theory and false according to the theory); (2) is just true according to the theology; and neither (4) nor (5) is true according to the theory (both are just false according to the theology).[26]

TOWARDS OTHER EXAMPLES OF CONTRADICTION

The principal focus, for simplicity, is the incarnation and the trinity, as above. But there are many other salient examples of contradiction in christian theology, some common to traditional monotheism in general. In the following sections, we discuss three such examples, each very familiar. As throughout, the aim is simply to illustrate the simple but abstract framework involving varieties of open and closed theologies.

10 Type C Contradictions: Evil

For the traditional omnigod contradictions, we utilize the Nagasawa categories (Nagasawa, 2008).[27] C-type contradictions are contradictions involving at least one property of God but also at least one property of non-divine things (e.g., humans). Thus, C-type contradictions often involve contradiction in both divine reality and non-divine reality.

Type *C3* contradictions are those C-type contradictions that involve exactly three of God's omni properties.

---

[26] Note that, as throughout, the background entailment facts are not stated in the theory itself but are truths or falsehoods according to the true theory of the target entailment relations. In the case at hand, (3) would be a falsehood according to the true theory of the given entailment relation.

[27] Nagasawa (2008) distinguishes between Type A, Type B, and Type C omni-problems. Our discussion proceeds in reverse order, starting with C-type contradictions, then B-type, and so on. What these types come to for Nagasawa is this: A-type problems involve only one *omni* property; B-types, two or more *omni* properties; C-types, one or more *omni* properties and some contingent bit of (non-divine) reality.

One of the most familiar C3-type contradictions is the familiar 'problem of evil', which involves three *omni* properties (viz., *omniscience*, *omnipotence* and *omnibenevolence*) and one contingency (viz., the existence of evil).[28] The contradiction is illustrated as follows.

1. God is omnipotent and God is omniscient and God is omnibenevolent.
   Source: three theological axioms; logical entailment from said three.
2. *Entailment fact:* That God is omnipotent and omniscient entails that God has the power and knowledge to rid the world of evil.
   Source: predicate entailment concerning omnipotence and omniscience.
3. God has the power and knowledge to rid the world of evil.[29]
   Source: (1) and (2).
4. *Entailment fact:* That God is omnibenevolent entails that God wants the world to be rid of evil.
   Source: predicate entailment concerning omnibenevolence.
5. God wants the world to be rid of evil.
   Source: (1) and (4).[30]
6. *Entailment fact:* That God has the power, knowledge, and desire to rid the world of evil entails that God rids the world of evil.
   Source: predicate entailment concerning power, knowledge, and desire/will.
7. It's true that God rids the world of evil (i.e., false that the world contains evil).
   Source: (3), (5), and (6).
8. It's true that the world contains evil.
   Source: empirical fact.
9. It's true that the world contains evil and false that the world contains evil.
   Source: logical entailment from (7) and (8).

11 Partial Theology: Responses to Evil

11.1 Closed under No Entailment At All

As in the other examples, a closed-under-none response affords an entirely unconstrained 'theory'. On this approach, all theological axioms reflected in (1) can be in the theology – and the rest of (3), (5), and (7)–(9) left out. Such an approach can fully embrace the standard background entailment facts (2),

---

[28] And to repeat, we are not endorsing or defending the given arguments. The driving service of this Element is illustration of basic tools and the overall framework.

[29] Suppressed here is that there's a logical entailment from (1) to both God's omnipotence and God's omniscience.

[30] Suppressed here is that there's a logical entailment from (1) to God's omnibenevolence.

(4), and (6);[31] it's just that the theological theory is not in any way governed by such entailment relations – including logical entailment, which, if the theology were closed under it, would otherwise put the contradiction (9) in the theory.

11.1.1 Historical Examples

We know of no historical examples.

11.1.2 Comment

The situation here is the same, mutatis mutandis, with the incarnation contradiction in Section 5.1. Such an approach to theology is tantamount to the pursuit of 'saying without asserting' or, perhaps, 'virtue signalling' whereby one just says or writes sentences that are entirely cut free from their standard implications, perhaps to signal that one is in such-n-so group of folks (though the motivation, in the present context, is irrelevant).

11.2 Standard Logic but No Predicate Entailment

On this approach, the theology is closed under so-called classical logic but otherwise unconstrained by background facts (2), (4), and (6). As a result, one variety of this approach contains (1), (5), and (8) without containing either (3) or the contradiction (9). Another variety contains (1), (3), and (8) without containing either (5) or the contradiction (9). When *logical* entailment is the only entailment relation under which the theory is closed, the given theology can contain all manner of claims without their standard (predicate) implications driving the theology to contradiction.

11.2.1 Historical Precedent

Here, again, perhaps epistemic-mystery accounts along the lines of Anderson (2007) or, perhaps, similarly 'analogical' accounts along the lines of Eschenauer Chow (2018) might fall under this variety of partial theology. On

---

[31] These are 'background' entailment facts in the sense that they are not in the theory; they are facts about relations that govern the theory's implications – or not, as in the closed-under-none approach.

A small technical note: The language of theology does not contain predicates for its various entailment relations, regardless of whether the theory is closed under them. The true theory about theology's various entailment relations is a separate theory that uses a distinct language. This is the same with the vast majority of true theories; it is in no way peculiar to theology.

such approaches, theology is closed under standard logical entailment (viz., so-called classical logic) but there's no 'knowable' predicate-entailment relation under which the language of theology is governed. Where predicates in the language of theology are 'understood analogically', there remains no identifiable predicate-entailment relation that governs their contents (to the extent that there is content at all).

11.2.2 Comment

The asymmetry of the given approach is at least a prima facie problem. Unlike the 'reverse' approach (viz., closed under predicate entailment but not under logic), the approach also cuts off the entailments of its central language – namely, theological predicates. If the theory's predicates are not constrained by their implications, it's at least prima facie curious as to the role of the would-be theory – perhaps, again, something along the lines of 'virtue signalling' or some such phenomenon, or simply a *tell just some but not all of the truth* sort of endeavour.

11.3 Standard Predicate Entailment Only

This approach contains (1), (3), (5), (7), and (8) without containing (9). Of course, on the standard story of logical entailment, (7) and (8) jointly logically entail not only (9) but *all* sentences in the language of the theology; in short, (7) and (8) jointly *logically* entail the trivial theology, at least for the standard account of logical entailment. But the 'virtue' of the running approach is to allow for theological claims that *would* logically drive towards the trivial theology *were* the theology governed by logical entailment – but it isn't.

11.3.1 Historical Precedent

The work of Dahms (1978), though not at all explicit about the current C-type contradiction, is historical precedent. In effect, the approach takes very seriously the standard predicate entailments of theological language; it simply cuts the theology off from *logical* entailments of the theory. In short, theology is closed under the standard predicate-entailment relation but not closed under the standard – *or any* – logical-entailment relation.

11.3.2 Comment

The situation here is the same, mutatis mutandis, as in Section 8.2.2. See also comments in Section 17.1, which apply.

12 Robust Theology: Responses to Evil

12.1 Standard Logic and Standard Predicate Entailment

This is simply the trivial theology, as throughout.

12.1.1 Historical Examples

There are none.

12.1.2 Comment

The comment in Section 6.1.2 applies in this case.

12.2 Standard Logic but Non-standard Predicate Entailment

This is the standard approach, with many different flavours of detail. Here, all of the work goes into rejecting one of the background entailment facts, either (2), (4), or (6) and, in turn, spelling out a weaker or otherwise different (possibly incomparable) predicate-entailment relation under which the theology is closed. Without (2), (4), or (6) the theology need not contain (3) or, respectively, (7). And without (3), (5), or (7) the theology need not contain (3), (5), or the contradiction (9).

12.2.1 Historical Precedent

As in other cases, this is a common approach. See Tooley (2019) for different flavors of this approach.

For but one common familiar example, the work of Plantinga (1978), wherein the standard (background) predicate-entailment fact (4) is rejected in favour of a weaker predicate-entailment relation governing 'omnibenevolence', serves as recent historical precedent. The work on this particular approach, as with any such approach, is not only in making explicit the non-standard predicate-entailment relation but in spelling out the relation over other relevant predicates of the language – such as 'omnipotent', 'omniscient', and, important in the Plantinga account, 'free will' and the like.

12.2.2 Comment

As with any version of the current response (viz., standard logic but non-standard predicate entailment), a sharp question is conspicuous: why the unflinching commitment to the standard story of logical entailment when, as mentioned in Section 6.2.2, the standard story of logical entailment was never formulated as a story of *logical entailment* (qua universal entailment relation governing logical vocabulary in *all* true theories); it was formulated merely as the story of the entailment behaviour of logical vocabulary in true mathematical theories. On the other hand, at least with the given 'problem of evil', it is difficult to see how a non-standard account of logical consequence might help. (See Section 12.3.2.)

12.3 Standard Predicate but Non-standard Logical Entailment

Since logical entailment is explicitly invoked only at (9) – and thereby leaving the contradictory pair of (7) and (8) in the theory – there are not a lot of options for a weaker relation of logical entailment (than standard, so-called classical) that affords retention of (1), (3), (5), and (8) in the theology without the theology being the trivial theology (i.e., containing *all* sentences of the language of the theology). As throughout, a so-called subclassical account of logical entailment in the vicinity of so-called FDE (see Appendix A) is a natural account of logical entailment. Along this line, the theology may contain all of (1), (3), (5), and (7)–(9) without collapsing into the trivial theology. For present purposes, we shall assume that this is the main avenue for implementing the current approach towards closing the theology under the standard predicate-entailment relation but a non-standard logical-entailment relation.[32]

12.3.1 Historical Precedent

There is no known precedent for this sort of approach, short of suggestive comments (in a footnote) by Beall (2023).

12.3.2 Comment

Perhaps one reason for the absence of historical precedent has nothing to do with whether, in general, glut-theoretic approaches to robust theology (i.e., robust theologies that contain contradictions but are not trivial theologies) are true with respect to some theological phenomenon (e.g., incarnation, maybe the 'stone' problem, etc.) but rather has to do with the problem of evil in particular. At least on the given derivation (viz., Section 10), the apparent problem is not principally a logical inconsistency (which, on the current approach, is just one of many logical possibilities); it's rather an unwavering commitment to

---

[32] This is not in any sense the only option but without going into a lot of technicalities the current option is the best for illustration.

(7)'s being 'just false'.[33] As Weber (2019) notes,[34] an outright rejection of the truth of (7) appears to be a firm starting point for standard christian thinkers. At best, the running glut-theoretic solution would result in the theology containing not only the falsity – and so, the logical negation of – sentence (7); it would also contain (7) itself, thereby stirring up no logical problem in the theory but rather a theory-independent clash with the theorist's (i.e., the theologian's) initial starting point.

Another way to look at the issue: just as christian theology (at least standardly) treats the *falsity* of God's omnibenevolence to be *explosive* in the theology (i.e., the truth of logically negating 'God is omnibenevolent' in a robust christian theology results in the trivial theology), so too with the *truth* of (7). If that's correct, then a theology that contains (7), even if it contains its logical negation (i.e., a theology according to which the claim is glutty according to the theory, that is, both true and false according to the theory), is the trivial theology – *not* because *logical* entailment reduces the contradictory theory to the trivial theory but because of further background entailment facts that the theology imposes.

---

[33] *An important technical though terminological note:* in glut-theoretic approaches to theology (or to anything), some sentences are gluts – both true and false. To be clear:

- Sentence *A* is *true according to a theory* iff *A* is in the theory.
- Sentence *A* is *false according to a theory* iff the logical negation of *A* (viz., ¬*A*) is true according to the theory.
- Sentence *A* is *just true according to a theory* iff *A* but not ¬*A* is in the theory.
- Sentence *A* is *just false according to a theory* iff ¬*A* but not *A* is true according to the theory.

Accordingly, the point here is that perhaps the absence of glut-theoretic approaches to the derivation in Section 10 arises from the fact that part of the starting point of standard theology is fuelled by a commitment to (6)'s being *just false*.

　Another terminological point for those familiar with the term 'dialethism' concerns the difference between a glut-theoretic account of something and 'dialethism' or 'dialethic' account. Sometimes, the terms are intended to be equivalent, but more often than not the 'ism' is used for specific philosophies within broader glut-theoretic work. In particular, at least as used in some works (Weber, 2021, §3.1.3.3, p. 96), the given 'dialethic' position carries specific implications about, for example, expressibility or 'metalanguages' or 'what can be said' (thought, etc.) or the like, implications that are not at all assumed by a merely glut-theoretic account of language or anything else. In short, there's no '-ism' in recognizing gluts involved in the true description of some phenomenon any more than there's an '-ism' in recognizing conjunctions involved in the true description of some phenomenon – or disjunctions, or etc. For further discussion and concrete illustration of the differences between glut theory in general and dialethism in particular, see Beall (2022).

[34] We should flag that Weber's discussion is not in fact directed at any extant account and contains some assumptions that are likely to be rejected by most – if not all – christian-theological accounts. Weber's discussion responds to various exploratory 'dialethic' approaches to certain theological phenomena, one discussed by Cotnoir (2018). Still, Weber's given discussion may help to highlight the absence of target glut-theoretic responses to the running example of contradiction.

Whether there is any viable glut-theoretic response to the problem of evil, whereby both God's omnibenevolence and the existence of evil are *just true according to the theology*, remains open.[35]

13 Type B Contradictions: Divine Inability

Type B contradictions are contradictions involving only *omni* properties of God; they are contradictions directly of God alone, not also of other non-divine beings (e.g., humans) or the like. (This is in contrast to Type C contradictions discussed in previous sections.)

Type *B2* contradictions are those B-type contradictions that involve exactly two of God's omni properties.

An example of a B2-type contradiction involves prima facie contradiction between God's omnipotence – understood as unlimited ability (or ability to do flat-out anything logically possible) – and God's omnibenevolence, which, on standard (predicate) entailment, involves a firm limit against an ability to do other than good. The contradiction is illustrated as follows.[36]

1. God is omnipotent.
   Source: theological axiom.
2. *Entailment fact*: That God is omnipotent entails that God can sin.
   Source: predicate entailment concerning omnipotence.[37]
3. It is true that God can sin (i.e., that God is 'peccable').
   Source: (1) and (2).
4. God is omnibenevolent.
   Source: theological axiom.
5. *Entailment fact*: That God is omnibenevolent entails the falsity of God's being able to sin (i.e., falsity of God's peccability).[38]
   Source: predicate entailment concerning omnibenevolence.
6. It is false that God can sin.
   Source: (4) and (5).
7. It is true that God can sin and it is false that God can sin.
   Source: logical entailment from (3) and (6).

---

[35] In unpublished work ('God, gluts, and evil', unpublished notes toward a neglected glut-theoretic response to the problem of evil), Beall discusses, without accepting, one potential avenue.

[36] To repeat, we are not endorsing the argument; we use it in the service of this Element's principal goal, namely to illustrate a general pattern of theological contradiction and the underlying framework of entailment relations involved.

[37] Sinning is logically possible. Omnipotence, again, entails the ability to do anything logically possible.

[38] As throughout, we use 'the falsity of God's being able to sin' (or the like) as shorthand for 'it is false that God can sin' (or the like).

14 Partial Theology: Responses to Divine Inability

14.1 Closed under None

As with other contradictions, a closed-under-none response results in a 'theory' closed under no entailment relation, and hence under neither logical entailment nor a predicate entailment relation. On this approach, both (1) and (4) can be in the theory without all of (3), (6), and (7) being in the theory. Likewise, (1), (4), and (6) can be in the theory without either (3) or (7). In effect, the theology is a grab bag of sentences unconstrained by its consequences.

14.1.1 Historical Examples

We know of no historical examples.

14.1.2 Comment

The situation here is the same, mutatis mutandis, as with the incarnation contradiction in Section 5.1.

14.2 Standard Logic but No Predicate Entailment

On this approach, (3) or (6) is dropped from the theory; the theory is instead equipped with (or governed by) no predicate-entailment relation – and hence no predicate-entailment relation that puts (3) or (6) in the theory. Without (3) or (6), the contradiction at (7) need not be in the theory either.

14.2.1 Historical Precedent

As with previous examples, there are no clear-cut historical works explicitly under this approach. On the other hand, as throughout, some responses carry the appearance of the standard-logic-only (no predicate entailment) family. See comments in Section 11.2.1.

14.2.2 Comment

The approach confronts the same issues discussed in Section 8.2.2.

14.3 Standard Predicate Entailment Only

On this approach, the theology is not closed under logical entailment but rather only under standard predicate entailment as reflected in background facts (2) and (5). Accordingly, neither (3) nor (6) need be in the theory, and hence the explicit contradiction (7) needn't be in the theory.

Notable is that, on the given approach, both (3) and (6) can be in the theology without the theology collapsing into the trivial theology. Indeed, even (7) can be in the theology without its collapsing into the trivial theology. So long as the theology isn't closed under logical entailment,[39] the theology can be logically contradictory without collapsing into the trivial theology – the theology that contains all sentences of the language of theology.

14.3.1 Historical Precedent

Precedent surfaces, though not crystal clearly, in the work of Dahms (1978). As in both incarnation-fuelled and trinity-fuelled contradiction, wherein standard predicate entailment governs the theory (theology) but the theology is not closed under logical entailment, Dahms suggests the same lesson for issues surrounding God's would-be peccability. (Dahms, in said work, does not explicitly discuss God's would-be peccability; he explicitly discusses contradiction arising from the combination of all of God's standard *omni* properties together with the existence or actual behaviour of Satan.)

14.3.2 Comment

The comment in Section 8.2.2, mutatis mutandis, applies in this case too.

15 Robust Theology: Responses to Divine Inability

15.1 Standard Logic and Standard Predicate Entailment

This is the trivial theology, since standard predicate entailment delivers the apparent contradiction (7), and standard logical entailment delivers the trivial theology (i.e., *all* sentences in the language of the theory) from (7).[40]

15.1.1 Historical Examples

There are no known historical examples.

15.1.2 Comment

The trivial theology, given standard theological axioms, is not only untrue; it's the paradigm of an absurd theology. This much, at least, is uncontroversial among relevant pursuers of robust theology.

---

[39] And, again, the non-robust-theology approaches, as we are discussing them, take logical entailment to be per the standard story (viz., so-called classical logic) whereby every contradictory theory collapses into the respective trivial theory.

[40] Of course, standard logical entailment also delivers the trivial theology from (3) and (6) together.

15.2 Standard Logic but Non-standard Predicate Entailment

Here, the theology drops either (2) or (5) in favour of some weaker predicate-entailment relation governing the target predicates. Without (2) or (5), the contradictory claims at (3) and (6) are not entailed by the theology.

15.2.1 Historical Precedent

One early precedent is Pike (1969). In effect, the idea is that, on the standard predicate-entailment relation, 'omnibenevolence' (as a sort of 'moral perfection') entails the inability to sin; however, on the target non-standard predicate-entailment relation, 'omnibenevolence' does not entail the inability to sin. In short, there are relevant (theological) possibilities in which an omnibenevolent being can sin; and there are relevant (theological) possibilities in which an omnibenevolent being cannot sin.

15.2.2 Comment

The comments in Section 6.2.2, mutatis mutandis, apply.

15.3 Standard Predicate but Non-standard Logical Entailment

On the target derivation logical entailment is explicitly invoked only at (7) via (3) and (6) together. The 'source' of (7) is so-called *adjunction* (whereby arbitrary A and B entail their logical conjunction $A \wedge B$). One option is to underwrite the theory with a so-called non-adjunctive account of logical entailment (whereby said adjunction is logically invalid); however, unless the logical-entailment relation also invalidates the pattern from both an arbitrary sentence A and its logical negation $\neg A$ to arbitrary sentence B, the theology is still reduced to the trivial theory from (3) and (6) alone, regardless of (7).

A natural option is to accept a so-called subclassical account of logical entailment, one in the vicinity of (say) FDE, sufficient details of which are in Appendix A. Along these lines, the theology is contradictory in the sense that the target claims (1), (3), (6), and (7) are in the theory but the theory is not reduced to the trivial theology.

15.3.1 Historical Precedent

Beall's work, while not explicit on the given derivation of (7), provides precedent for the running approach (Beall, 2021). In said work, *the incarnation* delivers God's ability to sin via Christ's human nature and the inability to sin via Christ's divine nature. (In no sense is it suggested that Christ in fact sins.)

15.3.2 Comment

The biggest hurdle to this sort of approach appears to be psychological or socio-logical (or both). The rarity of gluts – that is, true contradictions, true sentences of the form $A \wedge \neg A$ such as (7) above – in many true theories (e.g., true mathematical theories, true biological theories, etc.) primes a fallacious but common inference to the generalization that no true theories contain gluts. This, as a psychological or sociological fact, is a hard fallacy to avoid. What is curious is that theology, and perhaps especially (but by no means only) christian theology, has *long* carried the strong appearance of contradiction in its central claims of divine reality (and the human–divine intersection of God enfleshed). The dogmatic clinging to the standard account of logical entailment remains without good grounds, but it remains nonetheless. And to the extent that it remains any such glut-theoretic theology confronts a big (though merely psychological or sociological) hurdle.

16 Type A Contradictions: The Stone

An example of a Type A contradiction is the familiar 'stone problem'.

1. God is omnipotent.[41]
   Source: theological axiom (viz., God has no limitations beyond logical possibility).
2. Either God can create a too-heavy stone or it's false that God can create a too-heavy stone.[42]
   Source: logical entailment (viz., logical validity of $A \vee \neg A$, that is, of *Either it's true that . . . or it's false that . . .*).
3. *Entailment fact*: That God can create a too-heavy stone entails the falsity of God's omnipotence.[43]
   Source: predicate entailment concerning 'omnipotence' (viz., falsity of being able to do something logically possible entails falsity of being able to do any logically possible thing).
4. *Entailment fact*: That it's false that God can create a too-heavy stone entails the falsity of God's omnipotence.
   Source: predicate entailment concerning 'omnipotence' (viz., falsity of being able to do something logically possible entails falsity of being able to do any logically possible thing).

---

[41] God is omnipotent iff God can do any logically possible thing.

[42] A stone is *too heavy* iff it's false that God has the ability to lift it.

[43] We use 'falsity of God's omnipotence' as shorthand for *it's false that God is omnipotent* and so on.

5. It's false that God is omnipotent.
   Source: logical entailment from (2)–(4).[44]
6. God is omnipotent and it's false that God is omnipotent.
   Source: logical entailment from (1) and (5).[45]

17 Partial Theology: Responses to the Stone

Partial theology, as throughout, is per Definition 7.

17.1 Closed under None

A closed-under-none response results in a 'theory' closed under no entailment relation, and hence under neither logical entailment nor a predicate entailment relation. On this approach, both (1) and (2) can be in the theory without (5) or (6) being in the theory. Likewise, since it isn't closed under logical entailment, the theory can contain just (1), since (2) is forced into the theory only via (closure under) logical entailment (assuming, as we are, the standard account of logical entailment).

17.1.1 Historical Examples

We know of no historical examples.

17.1.2 Comment

The situation here is the same, mutatis mutandis, as with the incarnation contradiction in Section 5.1.

17.2 Standard Logic but No Predicate Entailment

On this approach, (3) or (4) is dropped from the theory; the theory is instead equipped with (or governed by) a predicate-entailment relation that invalidates the standard (predicate) entailment. Without (3) or (4) the contradiction at (6) need not be in the theory either. (It could be in the theory but isn't entailed by anything in the theory, and in that respect *needn't* be in the theory.)

17.2.1 Historical Precedent

We know of no historical precedent.

---

[44] $A \lor B$, *together with the fact that each of A and B entails C*, logically entails C.
[45] Arbitrary A and B jointly logically entail the logical conjunction of A and B.

17.2.2 Comment

The approach is one that acknowledges that elements of the theory entail contradiction but the contradiction is avoided by simply not putting such contradictions in the theory. The only consequences of the theory are *logical consequences*. But standard *logical* consequence, under which the theory is closed, won't deliver either (5) or (6) without background entailment facts (3) and (4). The comment in Section 8.2.2, mutatis mutandis, applies in this case too.

17.3 Standard Predicate Entailment Only

On this approach, the theory (the theology) is not closed under logical entailment but rather only under standard predicate entailment as reflected in background facts (3) and (4). Accordingly, any of (6), (5), and even (2) need not be in the theory, and hence the contradiction need not be in the theory.

17.3.1 Historical Precedent

Once again, Dahms (1978) serves as historical precedent, the result being a theology free of *logical* implications but full of (standard) *predicate* implications. In this way, the theory reflects the full, standard entailments of the language of theology except for the universal *logical* vocabulary (common to all true theories), which is unconstrained in the theology. In short, the entailments of theological predicates are contained in the theology, but theology need not contain its own *logical* entailments.

While Dahms, as above, is a fairly clear (though not explicit and, alas, not generally clear) example of the standard-predicate-entailment-only approach, there may also be precedent in other directions, notably the work of René Descartes. Descartes, on some accounts, likely would have been fine with the idea that God could create a too-heavy stone. For Descartes,

> 'omnipotence' is, literally ... having the power to bring about any state of affairs whatsoever, including the necessary and impossible. (Hoffman and Rosenkrantz, 2022)

where *impossible* is that which is logically inconsistent. Accordingly, 'eternal' or necessary truths like mathematical truths or the laws of logic are no less dependent on God's creative power (i.e., no less contingent) than God's creating the universe or the agents that inhabit it. Specific to matters of logic, Harry Frankfurt argues that, on Descartes's view,

> God was free in creating the world to do anything, whether or not its description is logically coherent. (Frankfurt, 1977, p. 42)

Whether Descartes truly fits the standard-predicate-only response or, under robust theology, non-standard-logic and standard-predicate, is for Descartes scholars to tell. Still, what is clear is that the presence of contradiction *in theology* (versus, e.g., mathematics) was not necessarily a problem for Descartes (so, his theory would need to be either absent a logical closure relation or closed under a non-standard logic).

17.3.2 Comment

The comment in Section 8.2.2, mutatis mutandis, applies in this case too.

18 Robust Theology: Responses to the Stone

Robust theology is committed to theories (theologies) that are closed under logical entailment and predicate entailment. In short, robust theology seeks not just the truth; it seeks the *full truth*.[46]

18.1 Standard Logic and Standard Predicate Entailment

This is the trivial theology that contains not only contradiction (6) but, in fact, *every* contradiction in the language of the theory, for it contains every sentence of the language of the theory.

18.1.1 Historical Examples

There are no known examples.

18.1.2 Comment

Nor should there be.

18.2 Standard Logic but Non-standard predicate Entailment

18.2.1 Historical Precedent

This is by far the most common route. For different flavours of this approach, see the Element by Mawson (2018).

For but one example, work along the lines of Nagasawa (2017) serves as clear historical precedent. Here, the standard predicate-entailment relations that give rise to the given contradiction are rejected in favour of weaker predicate-entailment relations (even if these are not explicitly spelled out), while throughout the theology is closed under the relation described by the standard story of logical entailment (viz., so-called classical logic).

---

[46] Seeking the full truth is compatible with never reaching it. Obviously.

Further back, and less clearly, the work of Aquinas (ST I, q. 25, a. 3–5) may fall under the current variety of robust theology, wherein he argues that gluts (true contradictions) are in fact impossible. As a result, to say that God cannot do that which is contradictory is not a limit on God's omnipotence; such actions do not highlight any lack of ability. Rather, 'an action is possible, in the relevant sense, if and only if it is consistent, that is, if it is not self-contradictory' (Pearce, 2011). Thus, according to Aquinas, one's abilities (regardless of omnipotence) are not diminished by the inability to do what is beyond the space of logical possibility.

Finally, as with the incarnation, there's a sense in which epistemic-mystery accounts, as elucidated by Anderson (2007), fall under the current variety of robust theology, but with a twist. Logical entailment is per the standard account (viz., so-called classical logic); theology is closed under logical entailment; and so the target predicate-entailment relation in theology is non-standard if theology is closed under a predicate-entailment relation. The twist is that which of the many candidate predicate-entailment relations governs theology (i.e., the true theological theory) is a 'mystery' – beyond our epistemic ken. (One can see why this sort of approach might figure under the standard-logic but non-standard predicate variety of robust theology but also equally under the partial-theological approach that closes only under standard logical entailment.)

18.2.2 Comment

See Section 6.2.2, for applicable comments.

18.3 Standard Predicate but Non-standard Logical Entailment

18.3.1 Historical Precedent

Any theory devoid of (2), such as that discussed by Beall and Cotnoir (2017), is a historical precedent.[47] In addition, instead of gap-theoretic responses along the lines of Beall and Cotnoir (2017), wherein premise (2) is taken to be 'gappy' (i.e., neither true according to the theology nor false according to the theology), dual glut-theoretic treatments – whereby the argument is sound but, being closed under a suitably non-standard logic (e.g., FDE per Appendix A), the theology is not the trivial theology – are other directions of response. Some such glut-theoretic responses are discussed by Cotnoir (2018) and (Beall, 2023, chap. 7).

---

[47] We discuss only those partial-theology options that involve standard logical entailment and standard predicate entailment. We set aside those 'responses' that claim *without detail* that (2) is not an instance of so-called excluded middle (of the form $A \lor \neg A$) because it is 'not even a (meaningful) sentence' or the like. (Should requisite details be spelled out, the response would not obviously be a historical precedent of the standard-predicate-only response.)

18.3.2 Comment

Glut-theoretic responses to A-type problems (e.g., the stone problem) entail the truth and falsity of only one *omni* property. Different *omni* problems might involve more contradictions involving more *omni* properties.

SOME COMMON OBJECTIONS TO GLUT-THEORETIC THEOLOGY

In the following sections, we address five common objections to glut-theoretic (robust) christian theologies. Many of these are discussed further by Beall (2021, 2023); however, we rehearse them here (though, in a truncated fashion) given their frequent occurrence.[48]

19 Objection: All Contradictions or None!

All contradictions are the same; ergo, all theological contradictions are the same. Accordingly, any acceptable glut-theoretic theology must accept *all* apparent theological contradictions as gluts – as true theological contradictions.

19.1 Reply

On the standard so-called classical account of logical entailment, all contradictions are, in effect, the same regardless of predicates involved. If the particular content of a sentence is measured by its consequences then every single contradiction $A \wedge \neg A$ has exactly the same content according to the classical account of logical entailment. (Arbitrary $A \wedge \neg A$ logically entails arbitrary B according to the classical-logic account.) Accordingly, any robust theology closed under classical logic is one in which contradictions are indistinguishable in terms of their content.

Things are different on a subclassical account of logical entailment such as FDE (which remains our principal example).[49] On this account, arbitrary contradiction $A \wedge \neg A$ does not logically entail arbitrary B, and so contradictions in general do not share the same content. One contradiction might *predicate-entail* something that another contradiction doesn't; indeed, one contradiction might predicate-entail the trivial theory (i.e., it might entail all sentences) while another doesn't.

---

[48] For the interested reader, a great many more general objections are discussed in the service of the particular glut theories advanced under 'dialethism' by Priest (2006).

[49] See Appendix A for a brief presentation of FDE and some of its well-known extensions.

A conspicuous question raised by glut-theoretic theologies, theories that contain some contradictions, does not arise in robust theologies closed under classical logic. The conspicuous question is: how are contradictions distinguished?

The question is not so much about *somehow* distinguishing one sentence from another. After all, even the classical story, which treats all contradictions the same (see above), can distinguish them by their spelling. (One is spelled 'Christ is mutable and immutable'. One is spelled 'Christ is omniscient and ignorant'. And so on.) The question, when raised (as it often is), is generally this: how do we tell the *true* contradictions from the *untrue* contradictions?[50] A robust theology closed under classical logic never faces this question, for all contradictions are the same and all are untrue – never in any true theory. Glut-theoretic theologies closed under logic are different.

What, then, is the answer? How do we tell the *true* contradictions from the *untrue* contradictions? Since each contradiction must be evaluated on its merits (since, contrary to the classical-logic story, the predicates in the contradiction make a difference to what the contradiction entails), the answer is very, very familiar: you do exactly what you do *any* time you're engaged in the systematic search for the truth. In particular, you consider whether the sentence itself (in the current context, the given contradiction) is true. Since every contradiction is a conjunction, you do what you do in the case of conjunctions: figure out whether the one conjunct is true and also figure out whether the other conjunct is true. That you're dealing with a contradiction doesn't change the required work: it's true just if both conjuncts are true. And both conjuncts are true just if... and herein falls the work of seeing whether the conjunction's particular predicates are satisfied and so on. In short, figuring out whether a contradiction is true is no different from figuring out whether a particular sentence is true in general. Finding the truth is hard. It always has been. It always will be.

20 Objection: Glut-Theoretic Theology Complicates the Search for Truth

The search for truth may be hard, but it's a whole lot harder with glut-theoretic theologies. All standard methodological rules of enquiry are thrown into chaos. We should resist glut-theoretic theologies.

20.1 Reply

Not so. What guides the bulk of rational enquiry – the bulk of truth-seeking enquiry – is not some magical algorithm that tells you whether you've got the

---

[50] See, for example, McCall (2019, 2021).

true theory. What guides the systematic pursuit of true theories are very familiar methodological rules of thumb. Like any important rule of thumb, the target methodological rules are imprecise; however, they successfully constrain the pursuit of true theories all the same. For present purposes, there are three salient methodological rules of thumb.[51]

20.1.1 Seek Logically Complete Theories

Systematic truth seekers don't just seek a true theory of the target phenomenon; they seek the *full* truth. One important and very standard methodological rule of thumb along these lines is just this: seek a 'complete' theory in the sense that *every* sentence A, in the language of the theory, is decided so that *either* A is in the theory (i.e., true according to the theory) or its logical negation $\neg A$ is in the theory.[52]

20.1.2 Seek Logically Consistent Theories

The natural companion to a 'logically complete' theory is a logically consistent theory. Another important and very standard methodological rule of thumb is this: seek a 'consistent' theory in the sense that there is *no* sentence A, in the language of the theory, such that *both A and* its logical negation $\neg A$ are in the theory.

20.1.3 Seek Simple and Natural Theories

Another very standard methodological rule of thumb concerns simplicity and naturalness. The rule, in short, is to seek simple and natural theories over more complicated ones. The rule is (obviously) imprecise but it nevertheless guides the search for true theories.

20.2 Summarizing: Rules of Thumb and Contradictions

Reality ultimately determines the extent to which the standard methodological rules of thumb are satisfied. Even with respect to very simple phenomena, reality may frustrate the satisfaction of all three rules. Witness, for just one example, the true theory of arithmetic, which, as Kurt Gödel famously showed, pushes back against the satisfaction of the completeness rule (van Heijenoort,

---

[51] Beall (2021, 2023) discusses such rules and the effects they have on particular (christian) theological contradictions.

[52] On a technical point, we assume throughout that all relevant theories are so-called prime theories, which basically means that they respect the semantics for logical disjunction; in particular, such theories contain a disjunction $A \vee B$ iff they contain at least one of A and B.

1967); Gödel showed that satisfying the consistency rule for arithmetical (and set-theoretic) reality comes at the cost of the completeness rule.

Theological reality, at least per orthodox christian theology, has long appeared to frustrate the satisfaction of all three rules. The example of the incarnation in §4 is but one conspicuous case. What's different in the case of some of theology's contradictions (e.g., the incarnation), unlike the case of arithmetical reality, is that the inconsistency comes directly from *axioms* of the theology (e.g., that Christ is divine and human), and so being 'incomplete' with respect to those axioms is a non-starter; it is to walk away from the given theory.

The question of *exactly when* to reject consistency over completeness, or completeness over consistency, or even simplicity/naturalness over either consistency or completeness, enjoys no easy answer or, for that matter, even a methodological rule of thumb. In the end, serious, systematic, and responsible truth seekers do their best in balancing the goals of consistency, completeness, and simplicity/naturalness. If there were an easy rule as to when one bucks one of the said methodological rules in favour of another, the truth of most phenomena would very likely already be in hand.

Glut-theoretic responses to theological contradictions should be measured like all others. One must weigh the theory against alternatives. Is one clinging to consistency out of an unmotivated clinging to the standard story of logical entailment? Is one clinging to both consistency and completeness at the obvious cost of simplicity/naturalness? These are not easy questions. They never have been. They never will be. All that can be done is to keep grinding on, pursuing the truth with competence, fairness, earnestness, and a clear head.[53]

21 Objection: Lacking Phenomenological Support

Belief that reality is consistent – versus having contradictions true of it – is an optimal certainty, akin to the belief that the external world exists. (Think of G. E. Moore and his hands.) Supported by our everyday experience of the world, it is palpably clear that reality is free of contradictory entities; to believe otherwise is borderline irrational, regardless of what the philosophy of logic might tell us.

21.1 Reply

Our phenomenological experience of the world does not always reliably track the true nature of reality. Certainly, empirically verified scientific theories such

---

[53] And what needs to be avoided is the stupid goal of winning a debate or 'apologetic zeal' or the like. Just seek the truth with honesty and competence. The waste of paper and airwaves perpetuated by those whose goal is somehow to convince a sceptic or win debate or the like needs no further comment.

as quantum mechanics and Einstein's relativity theory indicate that reality (at its fundamental level, as well as at its largest and fastest) is much different from what our phenomenological experience suggests. Theological reality, at least on standard christian theology, is vastly richer than quantum or physical reality, and so the expectation of 'phenomenological match' is likely misplaced. Moreover, inferring the truth of theological reality merely from the truth about non-theological reality has long been fallacious in standard christian tradition, a tradition according to which theological reality is largely known via revelation.

Sometimes the evidence bucks what our everyday experience tells us, both in the natural world and, much less surprisingly, in the divine realm. But we must follow the evidence.[54]

22 Objection: Logic Is Not Theology

Glut-theoretic solutions require a thorough understanding of esoteric concepts such as logical consequence, the workings of various entailment relations, contraposition, and more. But theology is not concerned with such matters. Theology, as an enterprise, seeks to deliver an as-true-as-possible description of divine reality (trinity, incarnation, etc.). And that – and that alone – should be the focus of the theologian, not a bunch of entailment-relation issues.

22.1 Reply

First, it is simply false that a mastery of esoteric logics is required to grasp (or, more importantly, embrace) the glut-theoretic solutions on offer in this Element. Indeed, minimally, the foregoing sections, in conjunction with Appendix A on FDE, are sufficient for such tasks. Second, it is true that theology is not logic; however, theology, like most truth-seeking endeavours, *relies on logic* – certainly robust theology. In fact, as witnessed in the derivations above, long-standing issues with the doctrines of the trinity and incarnation are the result of the given theological axioms and the various entailment relations involved.

23 Objection: Issues with Detachment

The cost of glut-theoretic solutions to perennial theological contradictions is the loss of the logical validity of apparently ubiquitous 'argument forms' (as they're sometimes misleadingly called). Specifically, the emergence of gluts in a theory (here, theology) entails the loss of material detachment (more

---

[54] For much more on responses to this objection, see Beall (2021).

specifically, material modus ponens, material modus tollens, and disjunctive syllogism). Of course, given the apparent validity of such 'argument forms' in many familiar true theories, the cost of adopting a glut-theoretic solution is greater than any value gained from such a solution.[55]

23.1 Reply

The logical *in*validity of material modus ponens, material modus tollens, and disjunctive syllogism does not undermine the *extra-logical* or theory-specific validity of such forms in all true theories. As Beall notes,

> Simply because one thinks that the true logic – the logic over the whole of one's language – is subclassical does not mean that one thereby has foresworn all use of the classical closure operator. (Beall, 2013, p. 755)

Extra-logical consequence relations, which build on top of logical consequence to add further theory-specific (often predicate-) consequences in a theory, often restrict the space of possibilities recognized by the theory's (extra-) logical consequence relation, often ruling out gaps or gluts from the theory's given space of 'theoretical possibilities'. For one example, standard (true) mathematical theories often rule out the logical possibility of gluts and gaps, as these are standard taken to be irrelevant to mathematical reality. Thus, a weak account of logical consequence does not mean that *every* true theory is governed by an equally weak (extra-) logical consequence relation.[56]

CLOSING TAKEAWAYS

Christian theology, qua truth-seeking discipline, has the same resources as other truth-seeking disciplines with respect to entailment relations and contradiction. One striking difference between christian theology and many other truth-seeking endeavours is that, while the latter often confront apparent contradiction, the former appears to reflect contradiction right at the core of its fundamental axioms. One can, as always, reject the culprit axioms; however, the christian theological tradition largely retains conspicuous ones (e.g., elementary christological axioms, or axioms governing trinitarian reality, on top of slightly less fundamental claims involving traditional *omni* properties, etc.). The biggest takeaway of this Element is that attention to entailment relations

---

[55] Page (2021) objects to Beall's glut-theoretic theology along these lines.

[56] For much more on the mechanics of extra-logical consequence relations, see the work of Beall (2015, 2021).

driving the apparent contradiction is not only necessary; it opens up options for understanding the potential content and boundaries of theological theories.

What is not discussed in this Element is the important idea of 'dual contradictions' or, in standard philosophical lingo, *gaps* between truth and falsity. The topic of this Element is contradiction (including *gluts* of truth and falsity), but another important response to apparent contradiction involves seeing them as 'mirror images' of gluts (which is what the more technical word 'dual' amounts to, more or less). Along these lines, Appendix B briefly but only briefly points to some ideas around gaps.[57]

---

[57] Restall (2004) provides relevant discussion of the duality of gaps and gluts – that is, of 'dual-contradictions' and contradictions.

Appendix A

Logical Vocabulary and Semantics

The aim of this appendix is only to highlight notable similarities and differences between FDE and the standard so-called classical logic.[58] Many more details, including notable relations between similar 'subclassical' entailment relations, are presented by Beall (2021, 2023) and Omori and Wansing (2017, 2019).

A.1 Main Similarities

What is important, by way of notable similarities, is that the standard 'classical' account and the given subclassical (viz., FDE) account of logical entailment are exactly the same with respect to basic building blocks (i.e., syntax), truth and falsity conditions (in effect, semantics or meanings of logical vocabulary), and the definition of *entailment* as *absence of counterexample*. These similarities are presented in Appendix A.3.

A.2 Main Difference

The main difference between the target subclassical (viz., FDE) and classical account of logical entailment is that the former imposes no constraints on the space of logical possibilities recognized by the relation, while the latter rules out two notable subspaces of such possibilities. Both accounts are the same on the *fundamental pair of properties* of all sentences, namely *truth* and *falsity*. For convenience, model these fundamental properties by the number 1 (modelling truth) and the number 0 (modelling falsity), in which case the accounts are the same on the set of fundamental semantic properties, namely $\{1, 0\}$. Said difference arises at the obvious combinatorial possibilities determined by the two given fundamental semantic properties:

- a sentence might have only the property 1 (truth);
- a sentence might have only the property 0 (falsity);
- a sentence might have *both* the properties 1 (truth) and 0 (falsity);
- a sentence might have *neither* the property 1 (truth) nor 0 (falsity).

The last two combinatorial possibilities are *logical possibilities* according to the subclassical account; the last two possibilities are ruled out of the space of logical possibilities by the 'classical' account.

---

[58] This appendix follows the presentation in the work of DeVito (2021).

Comment. We note that *logical entailment* differs from the many other (extra-logical) entailment relations in being entirely 'topic-neutral', and in taking no stance on whether basic (so-called) atomic sentences are true, false, or otherwise. On the surface, it requires some special argument to rule out the noted possibilities (viz., true-and-false and neither-true-nor-false), but any such argument, presumably, must invoke something special about a particular topic – something that is beyond the topic-neutrality of *logical* entailment.[59]

A.3 Summary: Syntax, Semantics, and Entailment

What follows is a brief but, for present purposes, adequate account of FDE qua logical entailment (or logical consequence), all of which should be read in light of the foregoing. Moreover, for simplicity and brevity we give only the so-called propositional or sentential language; the full first-order language is a fairly straightforward generalization and is available in a variety of sources (Beall, 2021, 2023; Omori and Wansing, 2017, 2019).

A.3.1 Syntax: Basic Vocabulary and Sentences

The syntax is exactly the same in both FDE and the classical account. The syntax is standard:

- Logical vocabulary:
  - Two unary connectives: truth/nullation (†) and falsity/negation ($\neg$).[60]
  - Two binary connectives: conjunction ($\wedge$) and disjunction ($\vee$).
  - *Defined material conditional*: $A \rightarrow B$ is defined to be $\neg A \vee B$.
- Extralogical vocabulary: sentential/propositional variables 'p', 'q', 'r' with or without natural-number subscripts.
- Alogical vocabulary: parentheses '(' and ')'.

The *set of sentences* is exactly the normal set:

- Atomic sentences are all and only the propositional variables.
- Molecular sentences are all atomics and, where A and B are any sentences, all strings of the form $\dagger A$, $\neg A$, $(A \vee B)$, $(A \wedge B)$, and – derivatively – $(A \rightarrow B)$.
- Nothing else is a sentence of the language.[61]

---

[59] One might argue that the given possibilities (gluts and gaps) are ruled out *by the very meaning of the logical vocabulary*, and in particular *the meaning of logical negation*. But this just is not so, as Appendix A.3 makes plain.

[60] Nullation is often omitted from the explicit syntax because, given its semantics, it is logically redundant; however, the symmetry and duality of the pairs of basic logical connectives are worth making explicit.

[61] Again, generalization to the standard first-order language (sans identity, which is not topic-neutral and, hence, not logical vocabulary) is straightforward.

A.3.2 Semantics: Truth and Falsity Conditions

Semantics, as usual, are given via 'truth and falsity conditions' for sentences, which are modelled by *truth-in-a-model* and *falsity-in-a-model* conditions, in general. In the propositional case, full-blown models are not really required; instead, simple functions or 'valuations' may be used. Accordingly, the truth and falsity conditions are given via *truth-according-to-a-valuation* and *falsity-according-to-a-valuation* conditions.

We follow the simple Dunn-style semantics (Dunn, 1966, 1976; Omori and Wansing, 2019) wherein the set of fundamental two semantic properties is modelled as $\{1,0\}$ and the full space of semantic properties (or 'semantic statuses') is simply the given powerset $V = \wp(\{1,0\})$, namely $\{\{1\},\{0\},\{1,0\},\emptyset\}$, where $\{1\}$ is the status a sentence has (according to a valuation) if it is only true; $\{0\}$ is the status when a sentence is only false; $\{1,0\}$ and $\emptyset$, respectively, the statuses of sentences that are gluts (both true and false) and gaps (neither).

The truth and falsity conditions are given in terms of FDE valuations which are all and only those functions $|\cdot|$ from the set of sentences into V that satisfy the following conditions (where '$1 \in |A|$' and '$0 \in |A|$' may be read, respectively, as 'A is true' and 'A is false'):

- Nullation (†):
    - $1 \in |{\dagger}A|$ iff $1 \in |A|$.
    - $0 \in |{\dagger}A|$ iff $0 \in |A|$.
- Negation ($\neg$):
    - $1 \in |\neg A|$ iff $0 \in |A|$.
    - $0 \in |\neg A|$ iff $1 \in |A|$.
- Conjunction ($\wedge$):[62]
    - $1 \in |A \wedge B|$ iff $1 \in |A|$ and $1 \in |B|$.
    - $0 \in |A \wedge B|$ iff $0 \in |A|$ or $0 \in |B|$.
- Disjunction ($\vee$):[63]
    - $1 \in |A \vee B|$ iff $1 \in |A|$ or $1 \in |B|$.
    - $0 \in |A \vee B|$ iff $0 \in |A|$ and $0 \in |B|$.

And the defined material conditional has the usual conditions (derived from its definition in terms of negation and disjunction).

---

[62] In the general first-order case, the universal quantifier mirrors the conjunction conditions in the usual way.

[63] In the general first-order case, the existential quantifier mirrors the disjunction conditions in the usual way.

A.3.3 FDE: Counterexamples

Let X be a set of sentences and A any sentence. A *FDE counterexample* to the pair $\langle X, A \rangle$ is any FDE valuation $|\cdot|$ such that $1 \in |B|$ for each $B \in X$ but $1 \notin |A|$. In other words, an FDE counterexample to said pair is an FDE valuation according to which everything in X is true (i.e., contains 1) but A is untrue (i.e., does not contain 1).

Comment. Note that the FDE account of 'counterexample' is exactly the standard (so-called classical) account: namely, you cannot go from truth to untruth.

A.3.4 FDE: Entailment

FDE entailment is defined in the usual absence-of-counterexample way. In particular:

Definition 16 (FDE entailment) *Let X be a set of sentences and A any sentence. X fde-entails A iff there is no FDE counterexample to $\langle X, A \rangle$.*

Comment. Note, again, that the FDE account of 'entailment' (or 'consequence') is exactly the standard (so-called classical) account: namely, absence of counterexample. The difference, of course, between the accounts comes at the effects of the difference in the space of logical possibilities. With more logical possibilities, one has more candidate counterexamples that can serve as counterexamples to would-be logical validities. For example, in the standard, 'classical' space, there are no possibilities in which either the semantic status $\{1, 0\}$ (i.e., glutty status) or the status $\emptyset$ (i.e., gappy status) appear. As a result, in the given 'classical' space, there are no counterexamples to patterns such as

$$\neg A, A \vee B \therefore B$$

where '$\therefore$' stands in to separate the set $\{\neg A, A \vee B\}$ from the sentence B. Because the 'classical' account cuts out the glutty possibility in which $1 \in |A|$ and $0 \in |A|$ the given pattern is valid according to given account. On the FDE account, where there are no (ad hoc) restrictions of the given space of logical possibility, such glutty possibilities serve to counterexample the pattern. In particular, consider any FDE valuation according to which $1 \in |A|$, $0 \in |A|$, and $1 \notin |B|$ (i.e., either $|B| = \{0\}$ or $|B| = \emptyset$). Similarly, such glutty and gappy possibilities invalidate other patterns, such as the derivative material modus ponens (e.g., where A is a glut and B is untrue, i.e., either gappy or just false). Indeed, given the 'vacuous' logical possibility (see Appendix B), there are no *logically* valid sentences, and hence no 'logical truths' (i.e., truths that are true merely in virtue of logic), according to the FDE account. (This is a virtue of the account, given that topic-neutrality is neutral with respect to what is actually true or actually false.) Though some might erroneously think that the logical invalidity of such familiar patterns is a devastating problem for the FDE account of logical validity, the actual validity of such patterns is in fact extra-logical – the result of theory-specific restrictions of the space of logical possibilities. (Again, true mathematical theories, or at least true standard mathematical theories, rule out the logical possibilities of gluts and gaps *not* as logical possibilities but rather as *mathematical possibilities* recognized by the extra-logical entailment relation under which such theories are closed.) Much more on these ideas are available in cited sources.

Appendix B

A Note on the Dual 'Vacuous Possibility'

The exact dual of the 'trivial possibility' is the 'vacuous possibility', wherein absolutely no sentence is true or false. In the trivial case, everything is true and false; in the vacuous, nothing.

This Element focusses on contradiction. The principal threat of contradiction for a would-be true theory is triviality: 'exploding' the theory into the trivial theory in the given language. The dual of contradiction involves 'gappiness'. Whereas contradiction brings a sentence and its negation together in a theory, the dual of contradiction (let us say *dual-contradiction*) pushes both a sentence and its negation out of a theory.

The principal threat of dual-contradiction is not absolute vacuity (i.e., a theory in which nothing is true or false); rather, the threat of dual-contradictions for any would-be true theory is *partiality* or *incompleteness*.

The aim of systematic, truth-seeking theories is not merely a true theory; it is the *full truth* about the target phenomenon. While this is sometimes impossible for a single theory to achieve (even in simple levels of mathematics), the goal remains intact.

Responding to apparent contradiction by inferring dual-contradiction is a long-standing practice in philosophy and, perhaps, in parts of science. The practice is equally available in theology, though its implementation depends entirely on the case at hand. For example, taking the focal example of the incarnation in Section 4, one cannot claim that the central axioms are gappy without giving up the standard theory; however, where central axioms are not involved, a gap-theoretic response to apparent contradiction is worth exploring.[64]

---

[64] In a different but not irrelevant direction, one *could* claim that theology is gappy – including the target contradictions – but instead invoke a non-standard account of *correct theories* whereby the correct theology is at least not false. This account allows for the 'correct theology' to be gappy so long as the contradictions within it (i.e., sentences of the form $A \wedge \neg A$) are neither true nor false. This sort of idea is largely unexplored, though briefly discussed by Beall (2023).

References

Anderson, James (2007). *Paradoxes in Christian Theology*. Waynesboro, GA: Paternoster.

Asenjo, F. G. (1966). A calculus of antinomies. *Notre Dame Journal of Formal Logic*, **7**(1), 103–5.

Beall, Jc (2013). A simple approach towards recapturing consistent theories in paraconsistent settings. *Review of Symbolic Logic*, **6**(4), 755–64.

(2015). Free of detachment: Logic, rationality, and gluts. *Noûs*, **49**(2), 410–423.

(2021). *The Contradictory Christ*. Oxford Studies in Analytic Theology. Oxford: Oxford University Press.

(2022). Review of *Paradoxes and Inconsistent Mathematics*, by Zach Weber, in Notre Dame Philosophical Reviews https://ndpr.nd.edu/reviews/paradoxes-and-inconsistent-mathematics/.

(2023). *Divine Contradiction*. Oxford Studies in Analytic Theology. Oxford: Oxford University Press.

Beall, Jc and Cotnoir, A. J. (2017). God of the gaps: A neglected reply to God's stone problem. *Analysis*, **77**(4), 681–9.

Coakley, Sarah (2002). What Chalcedon solved and didn't solve. In *The Incarnation* (ed. S. T. Davis, S. Daniel Kendall, and S. Gerald O'Collins), pp. 143–63. Oxford: Oxford University Press.

(2013). *Sexuality and the Self: An Essay 'On the Trinity'*. Cambridge: Cambridge University Press.

Cotnoir, A. J. (2018). Theism and dialetheism. *Australasian Journal of Philosophy*, **96**(3), 592–609.

Crisp, Oliver D. and Sanders, Fred (ed.) (2014). *Advancing the Trinity: Explorations in Constructive Dogmatics*. Los Angeles Theology Conference Series. Grand Rapids, MI: Zondervan Academic.

Cross, Richard (2011). The incarnation. In *The Oxford Handbook of Philosophical Theology* (ed. T. P. Flint and M. Rea). Oxford: Oxford University Press.

Dahms, John V. (1978). How reliable is logic? *Journal of the Evangelical Theological Society*, **21**(4), 369–80.

DeVito, Michael (2021). Divine foreknowledge and human freedom: Exploring a glut-theoretic account. *Religions*, **12**(9). www.mdpi.com/2077-1444/12/9/770.

Dunn, J. Michael (1966). The algebra of intensional logics. Ph.D. thesis, University of Pittsburgh.

  (1976). Intuitive semantics for first-degree entailments and 'coupled trees'.*Philosophical Studies*, **29**, 149–68.

Eschenauer Chow, Dawn (2018). The passibility of God. *Faith and Philosophy*, **35**(4), 389–407.

Frankfurt, Harry (1977). Descartes on the creation of the eternal truths. *Philosophical Review*, **86**(1), 36–57.

Geach, Peter (1980). *Reference and Generality* (3rd ed.). Ithaca, NY: Cornell University Press. First edition published 1962.

Hasker, William (2013). *Metaphysics and the Tri-personal God*. Oxford Studies in Analytic Theology. Oxford: Oxford University Press.

Hoffman, Joshua and Rosenkrantz, Gary (2022). Omnipotence. In *The Stanford Encyclopedia of Philosophy* (Spring ed.) (ed. E. N. Zalta). Stanford, CA: Stanford University.

Jedwab, Joseph (2015). Against the Geachian theory of the Trinity and incarnation. *Faith and Philosophy*, **32**(2), 125–45.

Lehmann, Helmut T. (ed.) (1971). *Luther's Works: Word and Sacrament*, Vol. 4. Minneapolis, MN: Fortress Press.

Martinich, A. P. (1978). Identity and trinity.*Journal of Religion*, **58**(2), 169–81.

  (1979). God, emperor, and relative identity. *Franciscan Studies*, **39**, 180–91.

Mawson, Tim (2018). *The Divine Attributes*. Elements in Philosophy of Religion. Cambridge: Cambridge University Press.

McCall, Thomas (2015). *An Invitation to Analytic Christian Theology*. Inter-Varsity Academic Press.

McCall, Thomas (2010). *Which Trinity? Whose Monotheism?: Philosophical and Systematic Theologians on the Metaphysics of Trinitarian Theology*. Grand Rapids, MI: W. B. Eerdmans.

McCall, Thomas (2019). Doctrinal orthodoxy and philosophical heresy: A theologian's reflections on Beall's proposal. *Journal of Analytic Theology*, **7**, 473–87.

McCall, Thomas (2021). *Analytic Christology and the Theological Interpretation of the New Testament*. Oxford Studies in Analytic Theology. Oxford: Oxford University Press.

McCall, Thomas and Rea, Michael C. (ed.) (2009). *Philosophical and Theological Essays on the Trinity*. Oxford: Oxford University Press.

Mortensen, Chris (1995). *Inconsistent Mathematics*. Dordrecht: Kluwer Academic Publishers.

Nagasawa, Yujin (2008). A new defence of Anselmian theism. *Philosophical Quarterly*, **58**(233), 577–96.

(2017). *Maximal God: A New Defence of Perfect Being Theism*. Oxford: Oxford University Press.

Omori, Hitoshi and Wansing, Heinrich (2017). 40 years of FDE: An introductory overview. *Studia Logica*, **105**(6), 1021–49.

(2019). *New Essays on Belnap-Dunn Logic*. Cham: Springer.

Page, Meghan D. (2021). Detachment issues: A dilemma for Beall's contradictory Christology. *Journal of Analytic Theology*, 9, 201–4.

Pawl, Timothy (2016). *In Defense of Conciliar Christology: A Philosophical Essay*. Oxford: Oxford University Press.

(2019). *In Defense of Extended Conciliar Christology: A Philosophical Essay*. Oxford: Oxford University Press.

(2020). *Incarnation*. Elements in Philosophy of Religion. Cambridge: Cambridge University Press.

Pearce, Kenneth L. (2011). Omnipotence. In *The Internet Encyclopedia of Philosophy* (ed. James Fieser and Bradley Dowden). https://iep.utm.edu/eds/.

Pike, Nelson (1969). Omnipotence and God's ability to sin. *American Philosophical Quarterly*, **6**(3), 208–16.

Plantinga, Alvin (1978). *God, Freedom, and Evil*. Grand Rapids, MI: Eerdmans.

Priest, Graham (2006). *In Contradiction* (2nd ed.). Oxford: Oxford University Press. First printed by Martinus Nijhoff in 1987.

(2014). *One: Being an Investigation into the Unity of Reality and of Its Parts, Including the Singular Object Which Is Nothingness*. Oxford: Oxford University Press.

Rea, Michael C. (2003). Relative identity and the doctrine of the Trinity. *Philosophia Christi*, **5**(2), 431–45.

(2009). The Trinity. In *The Oxford Handbook of Philosophical Theology* (ed. Thomas P. Flint and Michael C. Rea), pp. 403–29. Oxford: Oxford University Press.

Restall, Greg (1997). Paraconsistent logics! *Bulletin of the Section of Logic*, **26**(3), 156–63.

(2004). Laws of non-contradiction, laws of the excluded middle and logics. In *The Law of Non-contradiction* (ed. Graham Priest, J. C. Beall, and B. Armour-Garb), pp. 73–85. Oxford: Oxford University Press.

Routley, Richard and Meyer, Robert K. (1976). Dialectical logic, classical logic, and the consistency of the world. *Studies in East European Thought*, **16**(1–2), 1–25.

Senor, Thomas D. (2002). Incarnation, timelessness, and Leibniz's Law problems. In *God and Time: Essays on the Divine Nature* (ed. G. E. Ganssle and D. M. Woodruff), pp. 220–35. Oxford: Oxford University Press.

Tooley, Michael (2019). *The Problem of Evil*. Elements in the Philosophy of Religion. Cambridge: Cambridge University Press.

van Heijenoort, Jean (1967). *From Frege to Gödel: A Source Book in Mathematical Logic, 1879–1931*. Cambridge, MA: Harvard University Press.

van Inwagen, Peter (1988). And yet they are not three gods but one god. In *Philosophy and the Christian Faith* (ed. T. V. Morris), Vol. 5 of Notre Dame Studies in the Philosophy of Religion, pp. 241–78. Notre Dame, IL: University of Notre Dame Press.

(1994). Not by confusion of substance, but by unity of person. In *Reason and the Christian Religion: Essays in Honour of Richard Swinburne* (ed. R. Swinburne and A. G. Padgett), pp. 201–6. Oxford: Oxford University Press.

Weber, Zach (2019). Atheism and dialetheism; or, 'Why I am not a (paraconsistent) Christian'. *Australasian Journal of Philosophy*, **97**(2), 401–7.

(2021). *Paradoxes and Inconsistent Mathematics*. Cambridge: Cambridge University Press.

Acknowledgements

For valuable feedback, we are very grateful to an anonymous referee, who provided the sort of comments that are genuinely fruitful, the result of careful attention to the work, and the sort of feedback that would make philosophy and theology much, much better were the feedback typical of referee comments. (Alas, such comments are all too rare.)

For explicit discussion of this work at various stages, we are grateful to (in alphabetical order) James Anderson, A. J. Cotnoir, Greg Restall, and Yujin Nagasawa.

Cambridge Elements ≡

Philosophy of Religion

Yujin Nagasawa
University of Birmingham

Yujin Nagasawa is Professor of Philosophy and Co-director of the John Hick Centre for Philosophy of Religion at the University of Birmingham. He is currently President of the British Society for the Philosophy of Religion. He is a member of the Editorial Board of *Religious Studies*, the *International Journal for Philosophy of Religion*, and *Philosophy Compass*.

About the Series
This Cambridge Elements series provides concise and structured introductions to all the central topics in the philosophy of religion. It offers balanced, comprehensive coverage of multiple perspectives in the philosophy of religion. Contributors to the series are cutting-edge researchers who approach central issues in the philosophy of religion. Each provides a reliable resource for academic readers and develops new ideas and arguments from a unique viewpoint.

Cambridge Elements $\equiv$

Philosophy of Religion

Elements in the Series

A full series listing is available at: www.cambridge.org/EPREL

Printed in the United States
by Baker & Taylor Publisher Services